Almost the Only
BRIDGE
BOOK
You Will
Ever Need

• VOLUME TWO •

RANDY BARON

BRIDGE SUPPLY

Practice. Play. Teach.

PUBLISHED BY:

Baron Barclay Bridge Supplies
3600 Chamberlain Lane, Suite 206
Louisville, KY 40241
U.S. & Canada 1-800-274-2221
Worldwide 502-426-0410
Fax 502-426-2044
www.baronbarclay.com

ISBN: 978-1-944201-17-3

Cover design by Mary Maier
Text design and composition by John Reinhardt Book Design

Printed in the United States of America

To my parents and grandparents who taught me
almost everything I have learned:

Lolo, C.D., Min, Sol, Mollie & Eddie

• • •

To my beloved cocker spaniels who have been
loyal companions for almost 70 years:

*Duke, Blackie, Honey, Smotanto, Victor, Vickie,
Satori, Louie & Bodhi*

Contents

SECTION TWO
Declarer Play

SECTION THREE
Defense

Acknowledgments

To Larry Cohen for his kind Foreword

To Lee Bukstel, Verna Goldberg, Ralph Letizia,
Bill McAvinue, Jim Morguelan & Norman Morris
for their help in organizing and improving my writing

To Brent Manley for his brilliant editing,
making it appear that I am somewhat literate

To Frank Stewart for his frequent invaluable advice
and impeccable writing

To my friends who agreed to include an essay
which improved the quality of the book greatly

To John Reinhardt, the world's best book designer

To Jimmy Maier for being an extraordinary partner
for over 20 years and who has never spoken a single
unkind word to me (even when I deserved it)

To Mary Maier for the unique cover design

To my sister Bonnie and brother Gary who have helped
keep me as sane as possible for many years

The abbreviation HCP is sometimes used for High Card Points
"He" or "his" was used to make the book more readable.

"LHO" and "RHO" are abbreviations for Left Hand Opponent
and Right Hand Opponent.

Foreword

RANDY BARON and I shared many years when we were both working hard to establish our credibility and earn a living at the world's greatest game. He was the founder and president of Baron Barclay Bridge Supplies, as well as the main publisher of bridge books; I was an up and coming author, player and teacher. We always had mutual respect and enjoyed our interaction as we sold our products. Randy and Baron Barclay were an essential part of making me who I am today in the bridge world. Although he sold his company over ten years ago, I'm very happy to see that Randy is sharing his wisdom and experience with less experienced players. More importantly, we have similar priorities in focusing on everyone having fun, being ethical and making clubs and tournaments pleasant places for everyone.

Randy consulted with me on various parts of his book. As I read through it, I was impressed how he has focused on topics that really do make a difference in improving the reader's game, similar to what I have attempted to do in my writing. Competitive bidding, declarer play and defense are three areas where virtually every player has much to learn and his ideas are very logical. Don't make the game too difficult, spend plenty of time discussing your agreements with partner and don't be afraid to try something new.

His teachings are simple to understand and retain, so his writing is an easy way to add to your knowledge. A good example is my essay on "Negative Doubles" which is included. Randy really liked my writing on the subject, so it is one of the principles from the best teachers and authors in the world that are included. I'm glad to endorse his invaluable contribution to bridge with this book.

—Larry Cohen

Introduction

Thank you very much for acquiring Volume 2 of "Almost the Only Bridge Book You'll Ever Need." I appreciate it even more if you spent your hard-earned money on my work. As the airlines say (and probably don't really mean it sincerely), "You have many options and we are so glad you chose us." In the bridge world there are hundreds of books that you can buy; with so many worthwhile authors and teachers, I am really grateful that you decided to read mine.

Originally, this was going to be a 64-page booklet or 100-page book. Somehow my essays gradually expanded into over 500 pages, so I decided to divide them into two volumes. Now you don't have to employ a Sherpa from Nepal to carry around one cumbersome book, so everyone but the chiropractors out there should applaud this decision.

As explained in detail in Volume 1, my main goals are for you to enjoy the game more, make sure you and your partner treat everyone with respect, and play ethically at all times. If you improve your bridge ability and results, that's a happy bonus.

Have fun and good luck, Randy

Competitive Bidding

♤ ♡ ◇ ♧

ONE

Interfere with Precision Club Auctions Whenever Possible

"The art of war is simple enough. Find out where your enemy is, get at him as soon as you can, and strike him as hard as you can."

—Ulysses S. Grant

YOUR OPPONENTS open 1♣, artificial and forcing. Don't panic: rejoice. They have just tipped you off on your proper bidding strategy.

You may be disappointed to hear this announcement of adverse high card strength, but don't let it intimidate you. Stay alert for ways to throw sand in the gears of their high-powered bidding machinery. That's easier than usual when they open with a big club. To see why, let's review what their bid tells you.

1. Opener has lots of high cards. They probably have game; they may have slam. Game for your side is remote. *Therefore every possible overcall can be used for some defensive purpose; none need be reserved for seeking your own game.*

2. They are about to use their bag of clever bidding gadgets. Their 1♣ opening has consumed the least possible bidding space, leaving them maximum room for exploration. *And giving you maximum room for defensive calls.* You may identify a killing lead, find a good save, or disrupt their finely-tuned bidding system, easing them into an inferior contract.

3. Opener's bid has said nothing about the hand's shape. *Interference calls are safer than after a natural bid,* for your opponents won't know whether to double for penalties or seek their own contract. If they have a fit they should play in their suit; if they don't they should double and defend; *since they don't know, you have them up a tree.*

Three reasons to *bid immediately, as high as you can afford.*

Of course, you can't successfully interfere every time, but you can do so often enough to erase the competitive edge they will gain if you timidly crawl into your shell when they open 1♣.

Here's an example. South deals with neither side vulnerable, and opens with a Precision 1♣.

> ♠ Q 2
> ♥ A 9 7 6 3
> ♦ A 9
> ♣ A Q 10 4

SOUTH	WEST	NORTH	EAST
1♣	2♠	Double	3♠
?			

Now what should South do?

North's double shows 5–8 points, balanced hand, or any holding, 9 points or more. (They are using the method recommended by Charles Goren's out of print book, *Precision System of Contract Bridge Bidding*).

Probably South passes and lets North decide. North bids 4♣. What next? Should South raise clubs? Try 4♥? Pass?

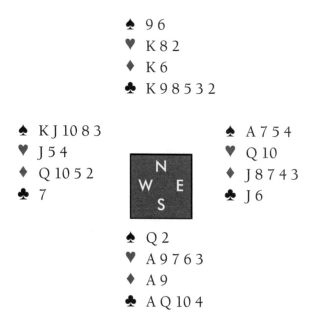

North-South's best contract here is 4♥, which is easily found if East-West remain silent, or compete only to 2♠. But after the 3-level interference, North may elect to defend 3♠ (for a 1-trick set), or South may guess 4♣ (missing game) or 5♣ (down 1).

If North shows up with fewer points in hearts and more in the minors, any game is a poor bet. Switch North's red-suit holdings and 5♣ is right; also swap one of North's spades for a diamond (or the heart queen) and the hands will make slam. Yet all these North hands would probably have been bid the same.

Now look at the East-West hands. No six- or seven-card suits, just one singleton — quite an ordinary holding. How did they safely find a 3-level preempt in two piles of junk? They knew how to seek a cooperative preempt. You can do it too, and your best chance comes when the other side opens with a Precision Club.

How High Can You Go?

You are probably used to thinking of bids as showing high-card strength. That's correct when you bid constructively, expecting to make your contract. With interference bidding, however, the important consideration is safety. You don't expect to make your contract, but you must stay below the level where the other side can score more by doubling and defending than they can make in their own contract. That's called your safe limit: the highest bid where the cost, if you are set, is less than the cost of allowing opponents to play at their best contract.

When You Can Take Risks

Sometimes you can risk interference beyond your safe limit, because your opponents are unlikely to penalize your indiscretion. You may go a half-trick into the risk zone when:

- *Opponents have not made a natural bid.* They won't know if they (or you) have a fit. If partner turns up with as little as x-x-x in your suit, their double will boomerang.
- *Opponents' doubles are not penalty doubles.* You may stretch a bit if a resulting double would be for takeout, or negative, or optional, or responsive. These are handy devices, but don't let the other side use them scot-free. Exact your toll by interfering with a lighter holding.
- *You are interfering at the 1- or 2-level.* They are unlikely to double when they'll have to take a stack of tricks to make it pay.

If two of the above conditions hold, you can stretch one trick. If all three are present, you still better stay within one trick (or rub your rabbit's foot).

When the distribution is wild around the table you can stretch one or two more tricks. (How far depends on how wild). On defense your aces may fall victim to their voids, and if they have a super fit, you do too.

When To Be Cautious

When the yellow flags are flying, stay within your safe limit, or even stop a half-trick shy. Here are the caution signs:

- *Opponents have made a natural bid.* Partner of the natural bidder now knows if they have a fit in that suit. If he holds your suit instead, you may end up paying from now until next February.

- *Partner has bid another suit.* You can't support partner's suit; partner is less likely to hold support for yours.

- *You are bidding 3♠ or above.* They have little room to find their best contract, so they are more likely to double and defend. If you overcall 1♣ with 4♠, you are practically forcing them to double. You better have the stuff.

- *Opponents are unlikely to have a major suit or notrump fit.* You judge this from your hand plus the bidding. With normal distribution, their minor suit fit will usually play at 3 notrump. When the gods give out singletons and voids, they'll have to reach for 5 in their minor to make game.

- *You're telling your opponents too much.* When you raise partner's interference call, you're telling the other side that you have a big fit. They can conclude that they must also have a big fit (somewhere), and set about to find it. An opponent with x-x-x in your suit can figure his partner for a singleton or void. You may drive them into a good game (or slam) that might be hard to bid if you simply stay silent.

- *You're telling them how to play the hand.* As a general rule, the information given by your bidding is at least as likely to help your partner as it is to help declarer. But be cautious about revealing a five-five two-suiter. If you end up defending, declarer will be able to place nearly every card.

When You Hold a Strong Hand

When they open a forcing 1♣ and you sit there with a strong balanced hand, pass. If they stop at a low level you can consider competing. That shows high card strength but denies the distribution values for an immediate overcall.
With a strong unbalanced hand, you bid to a sensible level, exactly as you would with a weaker hand. If partner has no high cards you have no game but you've jammed the bidding. If partner has a match you'll go to a makeable game and the other side may even double, thinking you are preempting.

When to Stay Discreetly Silent

You should not necessarily make a defensive bid, merely because you cannot be effectively penalized. You are also running another risk: you may help the other side find a superior contract, or assist declarer's play of the hand. If they have made only artificial bids, your overcall will usually pay dividends. But if they have gotten in a natural bid, you may not be able to inconvenience them at all, and your overcall, if any, should be directed at helping partner's defensive play.

Be cautious about raising partner to the 4-level when they have already exchanged quite a bit of information.

Other Ways to Interfere

Quite a few special bids have been suggested as ways to interfere with the big club. Here are other methods that have come to my attention:

- *Double for majors, notrump for minors.* This is the most common approach. Suit bids are all natural. A variant suggested by *Bridge World* magazine is to use double, 1NT and 2NT for 2-suiters excluding spades. (If you have spades, you bid spades).
- *Truscott 2-suit overcalls.* 1♦, 1♥, 1♠ and 2♣ each show the suit bid plus the next higher-ranked suit. Double shows hearts-clubs, 1NT shows spades-diamonds. In fourth seat, after a 1♦ negative, the meanings of double and 1NT are reversed, and 2♦ shows the red suits.

  Truscott was devised by Terence Reese and popularized by Alan Truscott. An interesting variant was suggested by Dorothy Hayden Truscott and endorsed by Charles Goren: use the 2-bids, double and 1NT to show a 2-suiter. This increases the preemptive effect and allows you to use 1-bids naturally.

  Truscott is most effective at favorable vulnerability. Saves and cooperative preempts are then common, making you anxious to show your suits right away, and the vulnerability gives you enough safe calls to show 2-suiters.
- *CRASH 2-suit overcalls* show either of two combinations with one bid. 1♦ shows suits of the

same color; 1♥, same rank; 1 notrump, same shape (pointed tops or rounded tops). You should be at least 5-4 in your two suits. The name comes from Color RAnk SHape.

- When partner makes a CRASH overcall, you'll often be able to blast to the 3-level right away, for while you won't know where your fit is, its existence will be certain. For example, you hold:

♠ Q 10 8 3
♥ 7
♦ A J 6 3 2
♣ 7 4 3 2

Partner overcalls 1♥ (majors or minors) and you jump to 3♦ (not vulnerable). If that's wrong, partner will correct to hearts and you'll re-correct to spades.

You can use any bids you choose as CRASH overcalls. The higher you go, the greater the preemptive effect — and the risk.

- *Baron over big club.* A bid of any number of spades bars partner from raising, for you may or may not have spades. What you have is either (1) spades, enough for the level you've bid, or (2) a one-suited hand in another suit good enough to play at the next higher level.

For example, if you have a one-suiter in clubs that you are willing to play at the 4-level, you could bid 3♠, barring partner, and then even bid 3NT when doubled, and then bid 4♣ to play. Sometimes you can even bid three other suits before settling into your real one.

The advantage of this is that it puts great pressure on the opponents, who can't tell where you intend to play. It also bars your partner so he can't cause you problems by raising your suit, or bidding when you know the appropriate level and suit. (If partner bids over your spades, it shows an excellent suit. Partner can weigh the risk against the gain).

Of course you can't risk this when vulnerable, for you then can't afford to bid a non-suit and have three passes follow.

RANDY: These methods were popularized in my booklet "Clobber Their Artificial Club," co-written with Ken Champney and Kit Woolsey.

TWO

Play Structured Takeout Doubles

"We all have to recognize that no matter how great our strength, we must deny ourselves the license to always do as we please."

—Harry Truman

THERE IS A RULE I never violate, as long as I have about 12–17 high card points when I make a takeout double. The rule is that I have tolerance for all three unbid suits. If you have 18 or more HCP, you don't need to have tolerance for all three unbid suits, because you can double and then bid again to show a strong hand. If you decide to violate this rule, it's a great way to get into trouble, because your partner will often bid the suit you don't have support for. You usually cannot resolve the problem, because when you have a normal takeout double (12–17 HCP), you shouldn't bid again.

Many inexperienced players (and even some who have been playing for a long time) violate this rule with hands such as:

♠ K Q 7 3
♥ K 9
♦ Q 9 4 3
♣ A 8 2

They make a takeout double after their opponent has opened the bidding 1♣.

Frequently, partner will respond 1♥ and now you have a real problem. If you bid again, it shows a stronger hand than you have, and if you pass, you may be playing in a suit with the opponents having more trumps than your side. There is a good chance you are in the incorrect contract and this can easily result in a disaster, or at best, a poor result.

The solution is simply to always have at least three-card support for any suit your partner may bid when you make a minimum/normal takeout double (12–17 points). Some books and teachers say that you should always have short-ness in the opener's suit (no more than a doubleton) and at least an honor in all three unbid suits. Well, sometimes you aren't dealt the perfect hand and I like to enter the bidding as much as common sense allows, so I relax these rules. If you have opening-bid strength and at least three cards in the unbid suits, that's good enough for me. However, this totally depends on what you and your partner prefer. Just make sure you discuss this so you are on the same page.

So what do you bid when you don't have a hand that qual-ifies for a classic takeout double? You have various options I'll discuss in more detail in this book. Sometimes you sim-ply have to pass, overcall with a four-card suit, or bid 1NT.

Here are some practice hands to make sure you under-stand this rule.

TAKEOUT DOUBLE QUIZ:

What action should you take when your opponent opens 1♥ or 1♠ and you are next to bid (neither vulnerable)?

1. ♠ 3
    ♥ K J 8 7
    ♦ A Q 4 2
    ♣ K 10 9 3

2. ♠ A Q 9 2
    ♥ 10 7
    ♦ K J 7 5
    ♣ A J 3

3. ♠ A J 10 7
    ♥ 4 3 2
    ♦ K J
    ♣ A Q 8 4

4. ♠ A Q 4 3
    ♥ 5 4
    ♦ J 10 8 5 2
    ♣ A Q

5. ♠ Q 5
    ♥ J 8 2
    ♦ A Q 5 4
    ♣ A J 3 2

6. ♠ 5
    ♥ A Q J 9 8
    ♦ A K 2
    ♣ Q J 9 5

7. ♠ 8
    ♥ A Q 6 5
    ♦ A 9 4 2
    ♣ J 10 4 2

8. ♠ A Q 8
    ♥ 6 2
    ♦ K J 5 2
    ♣ K J 8 6

9. ♠ K Q 9
    ♥ 8 5 4
    ♦ A K 6 3
    ♣ Q J 7

10. ♠ A 8
    ♥ K Q 8 6
    ♦ 6
    ♣ A K Q J 9 5

11.   ♠ K Q 10 4 2   12.   ♠ K 6 5
       ♥ A K 8   ♥ A 4 2
       ♦ 8   ♦ A Q J 8 7
       ♣ A 10 7 5   ♣ A Q

ANSWERS:

1. Over 1♥: Because you have a singleton spade, you should pass. Even though you have 13 HCP, it's better to pass and hope partner can bid or balance later in the auction.

   Over 1♠: A classic takeout double, just what partner expects.

2. Over 1♥: Double. Not only do you have a few extra points, but you possess 4 spades, the perfect holding in the other major.

   Over 1♠: Because you have only two hearts, a double is wrong. 1NT is the most descriptive call, even though you don't have a heart stopper. If you end up playing 1NT, that's not fatal and good partners put down a dummy with a heart stopper or two.

3. Over 1♥: Because you only have two diamonds, don't make a takeout double. Instead, make a four-card overcall of 1♠. You have a few extra HCP and if you have to play a 4-3 fit, it's not the end of the world.

   Over 1♠: Like Example 2, 1NT is the most descriptive call.

4. Over 1♥: A tough hand. Some players would treat the ♣A-Q as three-card support and double. That's tolerable, although not my style. That leaves a choice

of pass, overcalling 1♠ on a 4 card suit, overcalling 2♦ on a bad five-card suit, or bidding 2♥ (Michaels, showing spades and a minor) with 4-5 distribution (instead of 5-5, which most people promise). So there are five choices and every one of them has benefits and defects. I would probably bid 1♠ at the table, because it will probably get partner off to a good lead if we're on defense and four-card overcalls are OK.

Over 1♠: Pass or 2♦ are the only reasonable choices.

5. Over 1♥: Pass is the only option unless you decide to bid an Unusual 2NT with 4-4 distribution (not recommended).

Over 1♠: Your two options are pass or making a takeout double with only three not-so-great hearts. Depends on your style.

6. Over 1♥: I only have one spade, but I would bid 1NT, although I'm not thrilled about it. Pass is an option.

Over 1♠: Although I have at least three cards in the other three suits, I always try to overcall five-card suits, especially good ones. This is at the top of the overcall range for me. I wouldn't argue with anyone who makes a takeout double and then bids hearts.

7. Over 1♥: No alternative to pass.

Over 1♠: A classic double, even though you have only 11 HCP.

8. Over 1♥: Double. You would like to have four spades, but that's not what you were dealt.

Over 1♠: Pass is the only option, unless you choose to bid an undersized 1NT (if you're feeling frisky).

9. Over 1♥: Double. Even though you have three cards in hearts.

   Over 1♠: You can double, even though I prefer 1NT with 2 stoppers in opener's suit and such bad hearts.

10. Over 1♥: Double and see how the auction develops. You are close to making 3NT from your own hand.

    Over 1♠: Double. Partner might have four or more hearts and game is very likely.

11. Over 1♥: Double and bid spades, or overcall 1♠, depending on how aggressive you wish to be.

    Over 1♠: Tough hand. I would overcall 1NT, despite the singleton diamond, but I'm not thrilled to do so. No good alternative. A double can lead to many problems.

12. Over 1♥ or 1♠: Double. If partner bids the other major, you have a decision to make on how aggressive to be.

One more thought: Although it's not part of my system, some players use an agreement called Equal-level Conversion. When they make a takeout double of a major-suit opening bid, converting a club response to diamonds doesn't show extra strength. This allows a minimum take-out double of a major with short clubs, long diamonds and four-card support for the other major.

THREE

After Partner Makes a Takeout Double, When You Have a Bad Hand, Try to Discourage Partner

BY LINDA GREEN

> "Life is a festival only to the wise."
> —Ralph Waldo Emerson

I T'S NOT MUCH FUN to respond to a takeout double when you don't have many assets. This advice could save you when this situation occurs. When you have a four-card or longer suit and fewer than 6 points, your bid is usually automatic. It's a problem when your long suit is the one in which the opponent opened the bidding. If the auction has started:

LHO	PARTNER	RHO	YOU
1♦	Double	Pass	?

When you hold:

♠ 10 3 2
♥ 9 8 7
♦ K 10 3 2
♣ 8 7 5

You aren't good enough to bid 1NT. My recommendation is to never bid a three-card major, which could really excite your partner. Always bid your cheapest three-card minor instead; you hope this will slow partner down, so your partnership doesn't bid too much. If you switch the minor-suit holdings, so you have ♣K-10-3-2, there's no problem because you can make the obvious bid of 2♣. But when your alternatives are three-card suits, you just hope to escape without having a disaster.

In the March 2018 *ACBL Bulletin*, Jerry Helms presents a similar hand:

♠ J 4 3
♥ J 10 8 6 5
♦ 7 5
♣ J 6 5

After the bidding proceeds:

LHO: 1♥, Partner doubles, and RHO passes. He makes the same choice of 2♣ instead of 1♠, hoping partner will not bid too much. Jerry points out that a 1NT bid over a takeout double should show about 7–11 HCP with a stopper in the opponent's suit.

LINDA GREEN, originally from South Africa, is one of the country's top teachers, currently residing in South Florida. She is also an enthusiastic lecturer, professional player, author and director at clubs and on several cruise lines. Linda has participated in the World Olympiad several times and is a National Champion. Currently, she is Program Chairperson of the American Bridge Teachers' Association.

♤ ♡ ◇ ♧

FOUR

Light Overcalls Are Fun and Frequently Helpful

"If you opt for a safe life, you'll never know what it feels like to win."

–Richard Branson

THERE ARE TWO SCHOOLS of thought on bidding:

- You should have very solid values when you open the bidding, overcall or preempt
- You should enter the auction whenever you can

Many players stand somewhere in the middle of these extremes. I don't think there is a right or wrong philosophy; it simply depends on your personality and what feels right to you. It doesn't take a genius to realize that you are taking more risks when you have minimum values and choose to bid. You will suffer some setbacks and your poor boards will usually be blamed on you. On bad days, you might wonder why you stuck your neck out, and the negative results can be frustrating, even embarrassing. Look at the bright side: you can participate in more auctions, make life difficult for the opponents, and on a good day, the victories will accumulate hand after hand.

Let's look at the advantages and disadvantages of light overcalls:

ADVANTAGES:

1. It usually makes life more difficult for the opponents, especially in auctions when the overcall takes away a level of bidding. Overcalls such as 1♣–1♠, 1♦–2♣, 1♥–2♦ or 1♠–2♥ take away an entire level, giving the opponents less space to investigate. When you take away bidding space from the opponents, especially when they are vulnerable, they might be reluctant to bid. If you had passed, they have an easier call.

2. Your partnership may find a fit in your suit right away; if you pass, you may have a tough time describing your hand later or you may be shut out of the auction. You could even make a game or push the opponents too high.

3. Your bid may make it easier to find a sacrifice.

4. You might get your partner off to a helpful lead or help him avoid a disastrous one.

5. The opponents may evaluate their hands incorrectly and reach the wrong contract.

6. You may buy the contract at a reasonable level for a positive result whether making a partscore or a small minus.

7. When you don't overcall, your partner has valuable inferences in the auction and during the defense when the opponents play the hand.
8. Declarer may play the hand incorrectly, thinking you have more values than you actually do.
9. If you are playing against weak opponents, you may be able to steal the board.

DISADVANTAGES

There are only five major reasons for solid overcalls, but they are significant. I prefer light overcalls because I enjoy playing them, but there are certainly good arguments for solid overcalls. Disadvantages of light overcalls:

1. The opponents may double and you may be set for a (sometimes large) penalty.
2. Your partner may make an unfortunate opening lead.
3. You may give away valuable information to the opponents.
4. Because your overcall range is wider than with solid overcalls, your constructive bidding isn't as accurate.
5. You may go down in your contract for a poor result.

As they say, "Different strokes for different folks," so use whatever style of overcalls suits your partnership's personalities.

FIVE

It's Okay to Overcall in a Four-Card Suit When No Other Bid Is Appropriate

"Life is either a daring adventure or nothing at all."

—Helen Keller

WE HAVE ALL BEEN taught that when you overcall in a suit, you are supposed to have at least five cards in that suit. It's similar to when you make a takeout double over an opening bid of 1♥ or 1♠. You would like to have four of the other major...but sometimes that's not what you were dealt, so you have to do the best with what you have been given.

That's why there are some situations when you should make an overcall with a four-card suit. Such a bid can be very effective if you use it at the proper time.

One reason that I use four-card overcalls more frequently than most players is that I always use structured takeout doubles when I have a minimum. So unless I have at least three-card support for all of the other suits, I will not double. That leaves many auctions when my alternatives are to pass or make a four-card overcall. However, you should be disciplined when making this bid.

1. You should always bid only at the one level; two level overcalls are reserved for suits of at least five cards.
2. You should have a good suit, one that you would like your partner to lead if your side is on defense.
3. Your hand shouldn't be appropriate for a takeout double.

Four-card overcalls are underrated. Although they certainly don't work all the time, they take away valuable bidding space for the opponents.

They can also make the opponents evaluate their hands incorrectly. Each opponent could assume his partner is short in the overcalled suit, which might allow you to cash an extra trick when they play in a suit contract.

♠ ♡ ◇ ♣

SIX

Avoid Overcalling When You Can't Stand the Lead

"Speak only if it improves upon the silence."

—Gandhi

IT'S WINNING STRATEGY to be as aggressive as possible to make life difficult for the opponents. This creates a problem for many of us, because aggressive bidders like to launch themselves into the bidding whenever they can. They sometimes fall into the tactical error of making overcalls on weak suits. Although we like to enter as many auctions as possible, there is a happy medium when it comes to overcalling. Here is a typical example from Kelsey's "101 Bridge Maxims":

Both Vulnerable • Dealer North

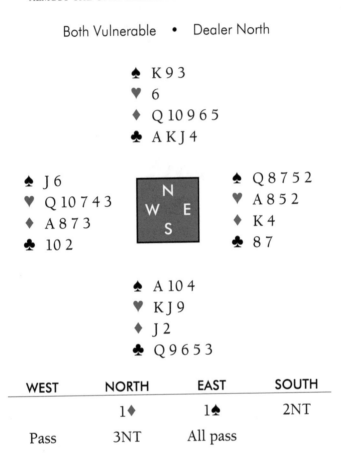

♠ K 9 3
♥ 6
♦ Q 10 9 6 5
♣ A K J 4

♠ J 6
♥ Q 10 7 4 3
♦ A 8 7 3
♣ 10 2

♠ Q 8 7 5 2
♥ A 8 5 2
♦ K 4
♣ 8 7

♠ A 10 4
♥ K J 9
♦ J 2
♣ Q 9 6 5 3

WEST	NORTH	EAST	SOUTH
	1♦	1♠	2NT
Pass	3NT	All pass	

Light overcalls are sometimes helpful, but they are likely to do more harm than good when they have no lead-directional value. In these situations, you can go ahead and bid, but be cautious, because you can bring your partnership a horrible result by your action. On this hand, the lead snatched defeat from the jaws of victory.

Respecting his partner's overcall, West rejected the natural heart lead in favor of the ♠J. Dummy's king won the trick, and although East played the discouraging ♠2, the damage had already sealed their fate. Declarer played a low diamond at trick two and the jack was captured by the ace. West now found the heart switch, but it was too late. South scored his king on the second round, entered dummy with a club, and finessed successfully in spades for his ninth trick.

At the other table, the normal heart lead held declarer to eight tricks. Note that on a neutral minor-suit lead, the defenders still have time to find the heart switch to defeat the game.

H.W. KELSEY (1926–1995). After spending many happy and productive years in the Far East, Hugh spent his later years in his native Edinburgh, where he was bridge correspondent to Scotland's national newspaper, *The Scotsman*. He represented his country many times in international competition and was twice champion of the Gold Cup, Britain's premier teams event. He wrote over 40 books on bridge, including the classics *Killing Defense, Improve Your Bridge,* and *The Tricky Game*.

RANDY: I had the good fortune to work with Hugh when we published *101 Bridge Maxims, Countdown to Better Bridge,* and *The Tricky Game*.

$$\spadesuit \ \heartsuit \ \diamondsuit \ \clubsuit$$

SEVEN

To Improve Your Competitive Bidding, Learn the Law of Total Tricks

"I am always ready to learn even though I do not always like being taught."

—Winston Churchill

THIS IS A GUIDE to help your partnership determine how high to bid when both sides are competing. Although this rule has been around for many years, it was popularized by Larry Cohen in his 1992 book, "To Bid or Not to Bid: The Law of Total Tricks," a classic that should be part of everyone's library. There is much more to the Law, but in its simplest form: In a competitive auction, bid to the number of tricks equal to the number of trumps you and your partner have between you. For example, if you have an eight-card fit, the two level is theoretically safe. If you have a nine-card fit, you can bid safely up to the three level and it generally applies to the higher levels also.

Although The Law was available previously, Larry's book popularized the concept. It has become the most used "rule" in competitive auctions. There is much more to his recommendations than blindly following this advice without making adjustments.

As discussed at length in his book, there are many adjustments that can affect your decision on how high to bid: how pure your hand is (aces and kings as opposed to queens and jacks), if you're vulnerable, how much strength you have in the opponents' suit, if you have a double fit, how solid your trump suit holding is, your defensive potential, and the ability of your opponents.

The total number of trumps is calculated by adding each pair's longest trump fit together. The total number of tricks available is the sum of tricks each pair can take if they play in their longest trump fit.

Here are a few typical Law of Total Tricks auctions. Playing five-card majors, how many tricks does each side have and what is your proper call?

Your hand is:

♠ A Q J 7 3
♥ 8 6
♦ 9 5
♣ J 10 6 4

and you are in fourth seat:

	LHO	PARTNER	RHO	YOU
1.	1♥	1♠	2♥	?
2.	1♥	Double	3♥	?
3.	1♣	Pass	1♥	1♠
	2♥	2♠	Pass	?
4.	3♥	Double	4♥	?

ANSWERS:

1. Total of 18 tricks…8 for them (5 + 3) and 10 for you (5 + 5).

   Bid 4♠ right away, especially not vulnerable. You can bid only 3♠ and wait to see what happens, but immediate action is better.

2. Total of 18 tricks…9 for them (5 + 4) and 9 for you (4 + 5).

   You could bid only 3♠ (reasonable when you are vulnerable), but I recommend bidding four, non-vulnerable, which is wrong only if each side has exactly 9 tricks.

3. Total of 16 tricks…8 for them (3 + 5) and 8 for you (3 + 5).

   Pass. If they compete to 3♥, partner should bid 3♠ if he has four-card support for you.

4. Total of 18 or 19 tricks…9 or 10 for them (7 + 2 or 3) and 9 for you (4 + 5).

   Bid 4♠. This is incorrect only if each side has exactly nine tricks.

♤ ♡ ◇ ♧

EIGHT

The Best Way to Play
Negative Doubles

BY LARRY COHEN

"Any fool can make something complicated. It takes a genius to make it simple."

—Woody Guthrie

IN MY OPINION, the Negative Double is the most important convention in bridge. It is made by the responder and shows enough to bid, with a hand not suitable for anything else. Responding on the two-level (after an opposing overcall) shows at least a five-card suit and at least ten points, so there is no good way to describe many hands. This is the reason the Negative Double is used. The chart below shows the only auction that starts a Negative Double sequence:

OPENER	OVERCALLER	RESPONDER
1 of anything	Any suit overcall	Double

In 1957, Al Roth called this bid the Sputnik, because it was as innovative as the newly launched Russian satellite.

Before he brought the bid to the masses, the double in the example was played as a penalty double. Even though Negative Double isn't a great name (maybe it should be called "Takeout Double by Responder" since there is nothing bad about the bid), it is used by virtually everyone today.

What Are the Requirements for a Negative Double?

The answer depends on how high opener will need to bid once partner makes a Negative Double. The higher opener has to go to respond, the more the doubler should have. Here are my recommendations:

- At the one level 6–7 HCP or more
- At the two level 8–9 HCP or more
- At the three level 11–12 HCP or more

The upper range is unlimited, so you can make a Negative Double with an opening bid or much more if this is the most descriptive call you have available.

Here are a few quizzes to test you.

After 1♣ by your partner and a 1♠ overcall, what would you bid with:

1.	2.
♠ 9 7	♠ 8 7 4
♥ A Q 6 4	♥ K 8 4 2
♦ K 8 6 5	♦ Q 8 6 5
♣ 7 4 3	♣ 8 3

3. ♠ K 7
   ♥ A J 10 9 6 4
   ♦ 6 5 3
   ♣ 6 5

4. ♠ 6
   ♥ K J 9 5 4
   ♦ J 7 5
   ♣ Q 8 5 4

ANSWERS:

1. Double. A classic Negative Double
2. Pass. You don't have enough to Double.
3. Double. You don't have enough to bid 2♥ directly, so the proper bid is to double and then bid hearts as cheaply as possible.
4. Double. You are a little light, but you don't want the deal passed out at 1♠.

After 1♦ by your partner and a 3♥ overcall, what would you bid with:

5. ♠ K Q J 8 7
   ♥ A 3
   ♦ A 7 5 4
   ♣ J 7

6. ♠ K 8 6
   ♥ A Q 10 4
   ♦ 6 5
   ♣ J 7 3 2

7. ♠ A Q 9 6
   ♥ J 8
   ♦ K J 6 4
   ♣ Q 10 9

8. ♠ A K 7 6
   ♥ 5 4
   ♦ A K J
   ♣ K 6 5 2

ANSWERS:

5. 3♠...You are showing five spades and at least an opening hand.

6. Pass...You cannot double, because partner will bid. Maybe he will reopen with a double and if he passes that should be all right.

7. Double...Aren't you glad you are playing Negative Doubles?

8. Double...Negative Doubles are unlimited...You first try to find a 4-4 spade fit and then see how the auction develops.

You have seen that I recommend Negative Doubles on the three level and I think they should be played for all overcalls. They make sense at the higher levels, because the higher they bid, the less likely you are to have a penalty double. So the only reasonable choice is to write "Through 7♥", "Through 7♠" or "Through Infinity." You'll also have some interesting and enjoyable conversations with your opponents about your card.

What does the Negative Double promise in the unbid suits?

The double is for takeout with the focus on the other major. With five cards in the other major and a good enough hand (on the one level 6+ HCP; on the two level 10+), the responder will bid the major instead of doubling. He will usually double if he has only four cards in the major or not enough strength to bid on the two level. The doubler doesn't promise both of the unbid suits, but he needs to be careful to have decent support for them.

A few further thoughts:

- If the bidding proceeds 1♦ – 2♣ ? and your hand is:

  ♠ 9 5 3 2
  ♥ A Q J 10 7
  ♦ Q 6
  ♣ 9 7

You shouldn't make a Negative Double, because if Opener bids a minor, it's likely to be a bad place to play. However, if Responder has:

  ♠ 9 4 3
  ♥ A Q 10 7
  ♦ K J 8 4
  ♣ 7 4

It's fine to Double, because he can bid diamonds if partner bids clubs.

- After a 1♦ overcall, the double promises at least four cards in both majors. Bidding a major promises only four in that major but there could be more.
- After a 1♥ overcall, a 1♠ bid shows at least a five-card suit. Double shows exactly four spades.

LARRY COHEN of Delray Beach, Florida has been one of the leading bridge teachers and players in the world for over 30 years. He has been named One of the Most Influential Bridge People of All Time, ACBL Player of the Year and Sportsman of the Year. His books and software have won seven awards from the American Bridge Teachers' Association. With his lovely wife Maria, he enjoys cruising and giving popular seminars all over the world.

NINE

You Might Like to Try My (Advanced) Methods for Negative Free Bids/Negative Doubles and Jump Shifts

"You may be right, I may be crazy. But it just may be a lunatic you're looking for."

—Billy Joel

ALTHOUGH I HAVE CAUTIONED everyone about using too many conventions (and especially those you don't discuss in detail with your regular partner), I do have a few bids that I really like that seem to work well for my partnership. They cover auctions when it is difficult to show specific hands, so I feel they make my life easier and that they have been worthwhile to include in my arsenal.

NEGATIVE FREE BIDS can be a helpful addition to your system.

Let's say the bidding has proceeded:

1♣ by partner, 1♠ by your opponent. It's your call with:

♠ Q 4
♥ A Q 10 6 5 2
♦ 9 6
♣ 8 6 4

You aren't strong enough to bid 2♥, so the normal bid is a Negative Double, hoping to bid 2♥ on the next round of the auction. However, the opponents may raise spades or there are other situations when you might not have a chance to bid your long suit comfortably.

If you are playing Negative Free Bids, the solution is easy. You can bid 2♥, which is non-forcing. This shows about 7–11 HCP and a six-card suit (or a very good five-card suit).

When you are playing these bids, Negative Doubles are no longer used for hands like the above example. They are needed for stronger hands, so a Negative Double followed by a new suit is now forcing to game.

Many partnerships use Negative Free Bids on the two and three level only; I play them on the two level and through 3♦.

The second bid I enjoy playing is my version of JUMP SHIFTS, which I call BARON JUMP SHIFTS. Almost everyone plays that the sequences when you skip the bidding one level during the first round of the auction such as:

1♦ by partner/ pass by the opponent/ 2♥ by me is either a weak bid (a six-card or longer suit with fewer than the 5 or 6 HCP usually needed to respond 1♥) or a strong bid (at least 17 HCP or more) putting your partnership in the slam range.

I have found when playing my beloved Precision Club that those very weak or very strong hands can be handled effectively with other methods. My preference is to use this bid for:

A six- or seven-card suit with 7–11 high-card points

The hands discussed in this principle (both Negative Free Bids and Baron Jump Shifts) are tough ones to handle when playing Standard American. It's hard to stop low enough and also to show partner the length of your suit. Although these bids don't come up often, when they do we usually land in the proper contract while the rest of the field struggles.

If you are an advanced player AND have a solid, regular partnership, you might want to give these bids a try.

♠ ♡ ◇ ♧

TEN

Three No Trump
Is Often the Best Contract
When the Opponents Open
with a Preemptive Bid

"There is no greatness where there is not simplicity."

—Leo Tolstoy

WE HAVE ALL HAD auctions when we tried 3NT as our final contract, went down, and realized that another resting place would have been more successful. 3NT isn't always the best bid, but when the opponents open with a preempt on the two or three level, 3NT is often the best choice.

There are several reasons for this:

a. Your bidding space is limited, so you don't have the luxury of exploring all of your options.
b. When you declare against a preempt, you usually have an accurate idea of the enemy distribution, so

the pathway to the winning line can be calculated more easily.

c. Sometimes the preemptor doesn't have an entry to his suit and you can keep him out of the lead by holding up. At other times, you have ways to keep him from running his suit by taking finesses and plays into his partner's hand.

d. 3NT is often a difficult contract to defend.

e. You don't have to worry about a bad trump split.

f. The opponents can't ruff your winning tricks.

♤ ♡ ◇ ♧

ELEVEN

Don't Hang Partner

"The strong person is the one who is able to intercept at will the communication between the senses and the mind."

–Napoleon

EXPERIENCED PARTNERSHIPS win consistently because they know each other's tendencies. Many pairs have a "pitcher" (the more aggressive partner) and a "catcher" (the more conservative partner). Other pairs have two more similar personalities during auctions. The more you play together, the easier it is to use proper judgment when you have to decide whether to compete further.

The important actions I'll discuss here are those situations when one partner takes a bid and his partner makes an unwise call. This is called "hanging your partner." It's crucial to understand when it is proper to bid again and when it's your obligation to pass.

Sometimes partner has to stretch to compete instead of allowing the opponents to win the auction. You should give him some leeway on these auctions. Don't punish him or he'll be reluctant to compete on the proper hands in the future.

Here are some of the actions that can hang partner if you're not disciplined:

1. Partner opens the bidding with a preempt. The opponents reach their final contract and then you decide to support partner. It's almost always best to bid the limit of your hand right away. Kit Woolsey discusses this in more detail in Principle #12, "The Last Guess."

2. Partner opens in third or fourth seat and tries to show a weak hand. You keep bidding and buy the contract when defending would be better for your side. Whenever partner tries to show a minimum or sub-minimum, be cautious.

3. Partner has entered the auction after an enemy preempt. He might have stretched to bid, so take that into consideration.

4. Partner overcalls. You raise him and then bid again. Instead of blindly competing, the one of the most important keys to the proper action is how many trumps your side has. The Law of Total Tricks is very helpful here (which is discussed in more detail in Principle #7).

5. You make a takeout double and then you bid again with the same minimum hand you started with. Leave it to partner, who knows your holding and don't compete further unless you have extra values (at least 15+ HCP).

6. Partner balances and you bid one more for a bad score. In this situation, make sure you have a really good reason to bid again. Partner has stuck his neck out and won't appreciate having it chopped off just because you want to compete further. Remember, when partner made his balancing bid, he was bidding your presumed values as well as his own.
7. You invite partner to bid game, he declines and you bid game anyway. Trust your partner and pass; he had the proper information to make his decision.

Make sure you understand the above auctions and don't take that extra push when you shouldn't. Your partnership will solidify and you will be successful more often.

♠ ♡ ◇ ♣

TWELVE

Try to Force the Opponents to Make the Last Guess

BY KIT WOOLSEY

"Bridge players exist mainly to make life difficult for each other."

—Omar Sharif

IT'S USUALLY A GOOD IDEA for your side to take up as much bidding space as possible early in the auction. If you can put your opponents in a position where they must guess what to do, then you have an excellent chance of getting a favorable result, because no pair can guess right every time. If you are the one who has to guess, the odds that you will be successful aren't great.

If you think it's correct to sacrifice in five of a minor because the opponents will probably bid and make four of a major, go ahead and bid it (assuming you won't go down more than the value of their game). When you watch the world's best poker players on TV, having their opponents make the difficult last guess on a hand is a valuable part of their strategy. The same holds true in competitive auctions at bridge. One of my pet peeves is when our partnership doesn't bid to its limit early in the auction and the opponents are allowed to find their fit in comfort.

Here's a typical example of the last guess:

You are vulnerable and the opponents aren't.
You are South and hold:

♠ A 4
♥ A K J 7 3 2
♦ 9 3
♣ K J 6

The bidding proceeds

SOUTH	WEST	NORTH	EAST
1♥	2♦	2♥	3♦
4♥			

Now it's up to West to decide whether to bid 5♦, likely as a sacrifice. It's a positive situation for you, because your auction is straight-forward. If West bids 5♦, you should double if you get the chance, because your 4♥ bid wasn't automatic. You took a chance and the opponents had to make the last guess. It's unclear what the final result will be: You might make 4♥ and you might not; the important point is that if they bid 5♦, you have an easy double. You made them make the last guess. That is winning bridge.

Here's another situation that occurs frequently:

Both sides are vulnerable and as South you hold:

♠ 8 2
♥ A K 10 8 5 4
♦ Q 10 7
♣ A 4

The bidding proceeds:

SOUTH	WEST	NORTH	EAST
1♥	1♠	2♥	Pass

Now it's back to you. Your options are to pass, bid 3♥ or 4♥. If you pass, it is very likely that the opponents will compete with 2♠ or another bid. You are unlikely to make 4♥, so that probably is not the best bid. However, if you bid 3♥, it puts the opponents in a difficult position. No one at the table knows exactly how many tricks are available for either pair, so East-West have the last guess. You are happy to bid 3♥ and put them to the test.

It's not always best to bid to the level you are willing to compete to, especially if you possess a higher-ranking suit than the opponents. Once you have decided you will compete further, it's reasonable to take the slow approach. You simply need to be sure how high you are willing to compete and that you are confident in your decision. Then they will have to make the last guess instead of your side.

E-W is vulnerable. You are South and hold:

♠ A J 10 8 5 3
♥ 6 5
♦ K J 2
♣ A 3

SOUTH	WEST	NORTH	EAST
1♠	2♥	2♠	Pass

It's up to you again and because your side has at least nine spades, the Law of Total Tricks tells you to compete to the three level. However, it makes sense to pass, because West might not have a clear action. He is vulnerable and may be fearful of competing higher. On a deal such as this, allowing them to exchange information is worth the risk, because you might be able to buy the contract at 2♠.

KIT WOOLSEY is a world-class bridge and backgammon player, analyst and author. He is a World Grand Master and he was elected to the ACBL Hall of Fame in 2005. I was privileged to edit and publish three of his classics: "Matchpoints," "Partnership Defense" and "Modern Defensive Signals." Kit lives in Kensington, California.

SECTION TWO

Declarer Play

♠ ♡ ♢ ♣

THIRTEEN

Think Before You Play at Trick One

"If you don't have time to do it right, when will you have time to do it over?"

—John Wooden, the greatest college basketball coach of all-time, a better human being.

A GREAT HABIT for any level player is to take awhile to play once dummy is spread. If you always take at least 10 to 15 extra seconds before calling for a card from dummy, you have given the opponents less information than if you simply play quickly when it's an easy contract and you hesitate when the hand is more difficult. Of course, there are some deals that take extra planning and that's perfectly fine. Just try to be consistent. If you have ever watched some of the top hold em' poker players on TV, almost all of them are very consistent in their initial action after they see their first two cards. You can certainly learn from these experts even though it's a different game.

This is especially important when you are playing against very good players. A talent most of them have is to watch what is going on around the table and use it to their advantage.

Taking extra time as declarer allows you to plan the play and also to consider what can go wrong. You might have several options, depending on what happens on the first trick or on other plays early in the hand. It's a good time to try to put into motion your best percentage play(s), as well as counting your winners and/or losers. Are you in the best contract, a reasonable contract or a poor one? Do you have a major problem on this hand? There are so many points to think about and a little extra time could enable you to take the best path.

It's not an easy habit to form, especially if you haven't practiced. Just try to make it part of your automatic routine. It certainly won't cost you and it may make a huge difference for you and your partner. It's best if both of you take this to heart and help each other remember this rule.

♠ ♡ ◊ ♣

FOURTEEN

Counting as Declarer
Is Essential

"It's not enough to have a good mind. The main thing is to use it well."

—Rene Descartes

AS I HAVE DISCUSSED throughout this book, counting is absolutely crucial to winning play. It's important to count your tricks in planning the play, before you play to trick one. You should calculate your sure winners, potential losers and what you know from the bidding about the opponents' HCP and distribution. There is much to consider and the more you practice counting to make it a habit, the easier it will be. We'll practice with problems that illustrate normal situations that you might face at the table.

To begin, let's look at a tough hand that would be almost impossible to make *without* counting the opponents' distribution.

1.

♠ J 10 8 6
♥ 6 5
♦ K 10 7
♣ A K Q 4

♠ A K Q 9 4
♥ A Q 4
♦ J 9 6 4
♣ 3

You reach an optimistic 6♠. The opening lead is the ♥7, solving one of your problems. East plays the ♥K, and you win. You draw trumps in two rounds, cash your ♥A, East following with the ten, and ruff your low heart in dummy, as East shows out, pitching a diamond. How many hearts did East have? Two, so West had how many hearts'? Six hearts. Suppose you continue with three top clubs, throwing two diamonds. Both opponents follow. You lead the fourth club, intending to ruff and make a diamond play, but East shows out pitching a second diamond. How should you play now?

East had only *three* clubs, so how many did West have? Five. What was West's distribution? Two spades, six hearts, five clubs...that's 13 cards, so West has no diamonds. If you ruff the fourth club and lead a diamond, you will be swiftly down. What is the alternative?

Right, you *discard* your next-to-last diamond on the fourth club. West wins, but he must lead a club or a heart; either way, you ruff in dummy and get rid of your last diamond!

Many less-experienced players consider *reconstructing the concealed hands* as something for experts only. In principle, this is a *simple* process, well within the reach of *anyone.*

To succeed at counting the hands, all you need are:

1. A little concentration
2. A little practice
3. The ability to count to 13

Counting distribution is based on obvious facts:

1. There are 13 cards in each suit.
2. There are 13 cards in each hand.

If you know that West has three spades, and you and dummy had four each, then East must have two spades. There are 13 cards in each suit.

If you know that West had three spades, four hearts and two clubs, then West must have had *four diamonds.* There are 13 cards in each *hand.*

The only problem is paying close attention to the play. That's where concentration and practice come in. Let's look at some hands and drill on counting the opponents' distribution. This will give you part of the practice you need.

2.
♠ J 8 4
♥ A 5 4 3 2
♦ 5 4
♣ K J 3

♠ K Q 9 5 3
♥ 7 6
♦ K Q 6
♣ A 10 5

You and partner have overbid, landing in 4♠ (but if you play the dummy well, you can afford to be aggressive in the bidding). West leads the ♥8 , and you win dummy's ace. You lead a diamond to your queen immediately, since you may need to ruff your third diamond.

West wins the ♦A, cashes the ♥K, dropping East's queen, and continues with a heart. East discards a club, and you ruff. You continue with the ♦K and another diamond, ruffed in dummy. Both opponents follow. Next you lead the ♠J from dummy. It wins the trick, as the opponents follow. So you lead another spade. East wins the ace, as West follows, and leads a diamond. You ruff with your ♠9, and West follows. So you play off your ♠K, drawing trumps. West follows, while East discards a club. All hands are now down to three cards. How should you guess the club suit?

Let's look at the evidence, suit by suit.

Spades . . . . .West had three. East had two.
Hearts . . . . .West had four. East had two.
Diamonds . . . . .West had four. East had four.

Clubs? You can work it out if you can count to 13.
West had two. East had five.

The odds are 5 *to* 2 that East has any particular one of
the missing clubs, including the queen. So you take your
make-or-break finesse through *East*. (A good declarer will,
of course, consider many factors in making a decision like
this. He may count the *high-card points* the opponents
show in the play. On this hand, the evidence of high-card
points is inconclusive, and declarer must rely on his *distri-
butional* count alone).

In the first two hands we discussed, the information
declarer needed to get a count fell into his lap routinely
during the course of play. But on many hands declarer
must actively seek to get a count.

3.
    ♠ Q 3 2
    ♥ Q 8 5 3
    ♦ A 10 2
    ♣ K 3 2

    ♠ J 7 4
    ♥ A K J 6 4
    ♦ K J 4
    ♣ A 7

You are declarer in 4♥ after West overcalled in spades. West leads the ♠A and follows with the king. East discards and ruffs the third spade. The ♣10 is returned, and you win the ace. You draw three rounds of trumps, finding that East got his ruff with a singleton trump. Now, before you make your diamond play, lead the ♣K and ruff dummy's club. You might get some useful information. As it happens, West follows to all three rounds of clubs, so your diamond guess is now a sure thing. West had six spades, three hearts and at least three clubs, so he has at most one diamond. (Remember, he had only 13 cards). Lead a diamond to the ace. If the queen does not appear from West, a finesse of your ♦J is bound to work.

Test Your Comprehension of the Material

1.
      ♠ A 3 2
      ♥ A J 3
      ♦ A J 10 4
      ♣ 4 3 2

      ♠ K 4
      ♥ K Q 9 8 2
      ♦ K 3 2
      ♣ Q 8 7

You are declarer In 4♥. West leads the ♣9. East wins the king and ace, and returns a club that West ruffs. You win the spade return and draw trumps. East follows to four rounds. Next you play the ♠A and ruff a spade, both opponents following. How do you play diamonds?

2. ♠ Q 3 2
    ♥ 2
    ♦ K Q 3 2
    ♣ Q 10 9 4 2

    ♠ A J 6 5 4
    ♥ 3
    ♦ 5 4
    ♣ A K J 7 3

East opened 1♥, you chose to overcall 2♣. West bid 4♥. North raised to 5♣, everyone passed. West leads the ♦J. East wins the ace, cashes the ♥K and returns a diamond to dummy. You ruff a diamond. East shows out, and draw two rounds of trumps, finding East with a singleton. How do you play the spades?

3. ♠ Q 10 8
    ♥ Q 3 2
    ♦ A J 2
    ♣ A K 3 2

    ♠ A K J 9 7
    ♥ 6 5 4
    ♦ K 10 3
    ♣ 5 4

You are declarer in 4♠. West leads the ♥J, and the defenders take the first three tricks in that suit and exit with a trump. You win and draw a second round, both opponents following. Now you play the high clubs and ruff a club. West shows out on the third club. When you draw the last outstanding trump, West shows out. How do you play the diamonds?

SOLUTIONS

1. East had five clubs, four hearts and at least three spades. Therefore, he had at most one diamond. Play the ♦K and a diamond to dummy's jack.
2. East had one club and two diamonds. He had at least six hearts (he would have opened 1♠ with 5-5 in the majors) but probably no more than six, else he might have bid 5♥. So East had at least three spades and probably four. You cannot hope for ♠K-x onside, so lead a spade to your ace, hoping that West has the singleton king. This is your only chance.
3. West had three or four hearts, two clubs and two spades. So he had at least five diamonds. The odds greatly favor taking the diamond finesse through West.

♠ ♡ ◇ ♣

FIFTEEN

Learn the Percentages When You Lack Other Clues

"The race is not always to the swift, nor the battle to the strong, but that is the way to bet."

—Damon Runyon

L ACKING ANY OTHER CLUES from the bidding or preceding play, a wise player uses the percentages when he has to locate a missing honor or set up a suit.

ALWAYS REMEMBER:

**An even number of cards
is likely to be divided unevenly.**

**An odd number of cards
is likely to be divided as evenly as possible.**

Thus, if you are missing four cards in a suit, they are more likely to be divided three-one than two-two. The exact percentages are:

3-1...50%   2-2...40%   4-0...10%

The only exception is when you are missing two cards: there is a slightly better chance that they are divided 1-1 than 2-0. The percentages are:

1-1...52%   2-0...48%

Number of Cards Outstanding

(All totals in this chart aren't exactly 100% due to rounding numbers)

2	2-0	48%	1-1	52%					
3	2-1	78%	3-0	22%					
4	3-1	50%	2-2	40%	4-0	10%			
5	3-2	68%	4-1	28%	5-0	4%			
6	3-3	35%	4-2	49%	5-1	14%	6-0	2%	
7	4-3	62%	5-2	30%	6-1	7%	7-0	1%	
8	5-3	47%	4-4	33%	6-2	17%	7-1	3%	
9	5-4	59%	6-3	31%	7-2	9%	8-1	1%	
10	6-4	46%	5-5	31%	7-3	18%	8-2	4%	
11	6-5	57%	7-4	32%	8-3	10%	9-2	1.4%	
12	7-5	46%	6-6	30%	8-4	19%	9-3	4%	
13	7-6	57%	8-5	32%	9-4	10%	10-3	1.5%	

There is an old bridge saying which concerns the proper play if you are missing a queen when you have the ace, king and jack of a suit.

EIGHT EVER, NINE NEVER

This means: With eight cards, missing the queen, a finesse is in order; with nine cards play to drop the double-ton queen. It is easy to see why you take a finesse when you are missing five cards, but with four cards out the percentages say that they will divide 3-1 mare often than 2-2. However, once both opponents have followed to the lead of the suit, there are now only two cards in their hands, and the percentages favor their being 1-1 rather than 2-0.

Always "PLAY THE PERCENTAGES" where there is no clue:

1. From the bidding indicating placement of honors or distribution.
2. From the opening lead indicating placement of honors or distribution.
3. From the play of the hand so far as to the placement of honors or distribution.

How do you handle each of these combinations, assuming that your opponent plays a small card at his first opportunity?

1. Dummy: A J 10 8
   You: K 6 5 4   _____

2. Dummy: K 7 6 5 3
   You: A 9 8 2   _____

3. Dummy: A 9 8 7 6 5
   You: Q J 10 3   _____

4. Dummy: A J 10 8 7
   You: K 5 4 3   _____

1. Play the king, then finesse the jack.
2. Play the ace and then the king (or vice versa).
3. Lead the queen; play low if it is not covered (unless your opponent is the kind who ALWAYS covers queens, in which case play the ace in the hope that your right hand opponent has a singleton king).
4. Play the king and then the ace.

SIXTEEN

Learn the Law of Restricted Choice

BY SHIRLEY SILVERMAN

"If you think education is expensive, try ignorance."

–Derek Bok

I N ITS SIMPLEST FORM: If you are missing four cards in a suit including the queen and the jack, and you are in a position to take a finesse after one of these honors appears on the first trick, you should do so. This may seem to contradict "Eight ever, nine never", but the odds are about 2 to 1 that the finesse is the winning play. One example:

A 10 6 5 2

4   Q

K 8 7 3

When you lead the K from the South hand, West plays the 4 and you play the 2 from North (the dummy), the Q appears from East. When you lead the second round of the suit from South (the 3) and West plays the 9, the best play is to finesse against the J in West hand, playing the 10 from North. You are hoping West started with J-9-4 and East with the singleton Q.

Here is a quiz from one of Shirley Silverman's texts, the most popular teaching materials for over 30 years.

THE LAW OF RESTRICTED CHOICE

If you are missing four cards in a suit, including the queen and the jack, and you are in a position to take a finesse after one of these honors appears on the first trick, then you should do so.

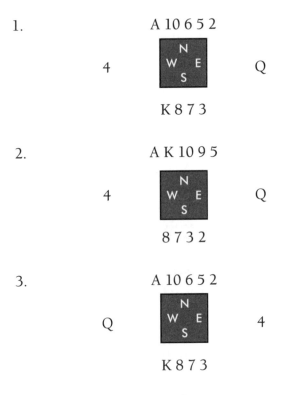

1.

A 10 6 5 2

4   N W E S   Q

K 8 7 3

2.

A K 10 9 5

4   N W E S   Q

8 7 3 2

3.

A 10 6 5 2

Q   N W E S   4

K 8 7 3

4.
                    A K 10 9 5

                    ┌─────┐
                    │ N │
         Q   │W   E│   4
                    │ S │
                    └─────┘

                    8 7 3 2

1. When the queen falls under South's king, should South finesse West for the jack?
2. When North's ace is played and East plays the queen should South finesse West for the jack?
3. When South plays the king and West plays the queen is a finesse possible for the jack?
4. When North's ace is played and West plays the queen is a finesse possible for the jack?
5. Why is a finesse not possible in numbers 3 or 4?

ANSWERS TO QUIZZES:

1. Yes
2. Yes
3. No
4. No
5. If West has a doubleton queen-jack, the jack will appear on the next lead of the suit. If East started with the jack plus two low cards, then a loser is inevitable.

SHIRLEY SILVERMAN (1928–1992) of White Plains, New York was an author, teacher, expert and administrator. She was co-owner of Barclay Bridge Supplies before it was sold to Baron Bridge Supplies in 1990. Shirley wrote many teaching books including her Five-Card Major series of Teacher's Manuals and texts, which have sold over two million copies since they were introduced in the 1970s.

RANDY: I will always be grateful for her support in my early years in the bridge supply business and her guidance when Baron and Barclay merged in 1990.

♠ ♡ ◇ ♣

SEVENTEEN

Learn the Important Card Combinations

"A little learning is a dangerous thing, but a lot of ignorance is just as bad."

—Bob Edwards

ONE OF THE WAYS you can really improve your declarer play is to study the various suit combinations that appear over and over. The exciting fact about these is that once you learn them, you should be able to recognize them throughout your bridge career. And even though there are hundreds of possibilities, you can learn the ones that appear frequently without too much work. It's simple to take the 13 cards in a suit and set up the card combinations as though you are playing at the club.

There are many ways to improve:

- Alan Truscott's *Standard Plays of Card Combinations on Flash Cards* (which I edited many years ago) includes over 100 of the plays everyone should know. This set will make the plays automatic if you take the time to commit them to memory.

- If you have the "Encyclopedia of Bridge" available, it contains virtually every combination imaginable. You can look at a few at a time or find the combination you struggled with at today's game to learn the proper play.
- My favorite titles include a number of very helpful books on declarer play and suit combinations. Some of the best and easiest to understand are Mike Lawrence's "Card Combinations" (obviously), Bill Root's "Play of the Hand", Barbara Seagram's "25 Ways to Take More Tricks" and Dorothy Truscott's "Winning Declarer Play." These authors are excellent teachers. There is a new advanced book on the subject, "Playing Suit Combinations" by Fred Gitelman and Jeff Rubens.
- There are also a number of excellent computer programs that focus on suit combinations and play of the hand such as:

Bridge Master 2000 Audrey Grant
Declarer Play at Bridge Barbara Seagram & David Bird
Planning the Play of a Bridge Hand Seagram & Bird
Play Bridge with Eddie Kantar
The Real Deal by Larry Cohen
Topics in Declarer Play Eddie Kantar

Here are some examples and quizzes to test your card combination skills:

♠ A Q x
♥ K x x x x
♦ Q x x
♣ Q 10

♠ K J x
♥ A x
♦ K J x
♣ A K x x x

You have reached 6NT, and the opening lead is a diamond. The ace wins on your right and a diamond is returned. To make this contract, you need five tricks from clubs. **Should you lead a club to dummy's ten or play off your high clubs, hoping for an even split?**

A 3-3 club break is less than an even chance, about 36% in fact. A finesse of the ♣10, on the other hand, will produce five tricks whenever the jack is on your left, provided the suit splits no worse than 4-2. The odds are only a little less than the 50-50 chance of the winning finesse. So the finesse of the ♣10 is best.

Throughout this book, we have talked about establishing tricks. In this principle, we will look at how certain common combinations of cards are handled to best advantage.

1. As seen above, you may need to know the *best percentage play* to win the *maximum* number of tricks in a suit.
2. With certain card combinations, *correct play will assure* the maximum number of tricks.

For instance, with:

A 10 x x   opposite   K Q 9 x x

play the king or queen first. You take five tricks even if either opponent has all the missing cards. If you carelessly cash the ace first, you will lose a trick if you find:

A 10 x x

J x x x 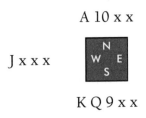

K Q 9 x x

The techniques involved here have been called "security" plays.

3. You may need to insure only a certain number of tricks. A "safety" play is like an insurance policy. You may give up the best play for the maximum number of tricks but you guard against losing tricks you cannot afford. Look at this example:

A Q x x x

x x x x

If you need five tricks from this suit, you must finesse the queen, hoping for the doubleton king onside. But suppose you need only four tricks. Let's say this is your trump suit in a small slam, and you have no losers outside of trumps. What should you do? You should cash the trump ace before leading toward the queen. You make your four tricks whenever possible (if your right-hand opponent has K-J-x or K-10-x, you can't avoid defeat), and you avoid the embarrassment of losing a first-round finesse to the singleton king and losing another trick later (at match-points whether to make a safety play is more complicated).

Obviously, you must count your tricks so you will know whether to play safe or for the maximum.

In each example below, assume that the bidding and play have provided no information to influence how you attack the suit. Entries are plentiful, unless otherwise stated.

1. A J 10
   x x x

   TWO tricks. Lead low to the jack. If that loses, lead low to the ten next.

2. A J 1 0 x x
   x x x x

   FOUR tricks. It is better to double finesse. Playing the ace first is almost as good.

3. A J 10 x x x
   x x x x

   FIVE tricks. Lead low to the jack (if left-hand opponent plays low). This is a "security" play which guards against K-Q-x on your left.

4. A K J 10 x
   x x x

   FIVE tricks. Cash the ace or king, in case right-hand opponent has the singleton queen. Then lead low to the jack.

5. A K J x x
   x x x x

   FIVE tricks. This is the old "eight-ever, nine-never" position. It is fractionally better to play off the ace and king.

6. A Q 10 THREE tricks. Lead low to the ten,
  x x x hoping that both the king and jack
     are onside.

7. A Q 9 x x FIVE tricks. It is best to finesse for
  J x x x x a missing king with up to ten cards
     in your suit. Be careful to lead the
     jack in case your left-hand opponent
     holds K-10-x.

8. A K J 10 x x SIX tricks. Take a first round finesse
  x x to the jack or ten. You lose to the
     singleton queen offside, but you gain
     if right-hand opponent has a small
     singleton, which is four times more
     likely.

9. A x x x THREE tricks. Lead the queen and
  Q 10 9 8 duck if it isn't covered. If it loses
     to the king, lead the eight next and
     duck it.

10. A x x x THREE tricks. Play the ace and lead
  Q 10 x x low toward your hand. If right-hand
     opponent plays low, your percentage
     play is the ten, winning if right-hand
     opponent has K-J-x-x. You cannot
     double-finesse as in the last example,
     since you lack good intermediates.

In each of the following card combinations, what is the best play for the number of tricks indicated? There may be more than one problem to each card combination. Assume that the bidding and play have given no useful information. Entries are plentiful.

1. A K 10 x x
   J x x x
   FIVE tricks

2. A x x x
   Q J x x
   THREE tricks

3. A J x x
   10 x x x
   THREE tricks, TWO tricks

4. A K 10
   x x x
   THREE tricks

5. K 10 9 8
   x x x x
   TWO tricks

6. Q 10 x
   x x x
   ONE trick

7. A J x x
   K 9 x x
   FOUR tricks, THREE tricks

8. A Q 9
   J x x
   THREE tricks

9. ♠ A J x x   ♠ x
   ♥ x   ♥ K J 10 x x x x
   ♦ K x x   ♦ A x
   ♣ Q x x x x   ♣ x x

You opened 4♥ as dealer and all passed. The opening lead is the ♠10 and you win dummy's ace. How do you play the trumps?

SOLUTIONS:

1. Play the ace and king.
2. Play the ace and lead low toward the queen-jack.
3. THREE tricks — lead low to the jack. If it loses, play the ace next.
   TWO tricks — play the ace and lead toward the ten.
4. Lead low to the ten, hoping the queen and jack are both onside.
5. Lead low to the eight. If that loses to the queen or jack, lead low to the nine next.
6. Lead to the ten. If the ace or king wins on your right, lead to the queen next.
7. FOUR tricks — lead low to the jack.
   THREE tricks — lead the ace and low toward your hand, planning to play the nine if right-hand opponent follows low on the second round. If left-hand opponent can win this trick, the suit has split evenly. If right-hand opponent has a singleton, win the king on the second lead and lead back toward the jack. This safety play guards against Q-10-x-x with either opponent.
8. Lead the jack; if it is covered, finesse the nine.
9. Lead a heart to your *king*. This is a guess in principle, but you will gain by playing the king if left-hand opponent has the singleton queen. If left-hand opponent has the singleton ace, you will always lose two tricks.

♠ ♡ ◇ ♣

EIGHTEEN

Learn Avoidance Plays to Keep the Dangerous Opponent Off Lead

"Danger and delight grow on one stalk."

—English proverb

IT IS NOT UNCOMMON for declarer to have to know how to keep a particular opponent off lead. This is a skill that cannot be overrated and with some study, you should be able to recognize these situations.

When you find yourself playing a contract where one defender can beat your contract or put it in jeopardy while the other defender cannot cause you such problems, it makes absolute sense to lose a trick to the safe opponent whenever possible.

One of the names for this dangerous defender that I really like is the "hyena", although I have heard him called other animal names that can put you in extreme danger. Think of the other opponent as the safe one to lose a trick to, while the hyena should be avoided at all costs if possible.

You'll be able to understand this concept better with these example hands.

1.

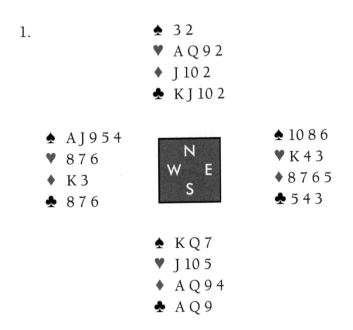

♠ 3 2
♥ A Q 9 2
♦ J 10 2
♣ K J 10 2

♠ A J 9 5 4
♥ 8 7 6
♦ K 3
♣ 8 7 6

♠ 10 8 6
♥ K 4 3
♦ 8 7 6 5
♣ 5 4 3

♠ K Q 7
♥ J 10 5
♦ A Q 9 4
♣ A Q 9

SUGGESTED BIDDING: South deals and opens 1NT. North responds 2♦ (Stayman). South rebids 2♣ (no major). North jumps to 3NT.

OPENING LEAD: ♠5

THE PLAY: Declarer wins the first trick and should realize that West has led from a spade suit headed by the ace and is now lurking behind him with a "tenace" holding in spades. It will be fatal to allow East to win a trick and lead spades through. So declarer leads a club to dummy and takes the diamond finesse. It can only lose to West who can do no damage. At least nine tricks are assured.

2.

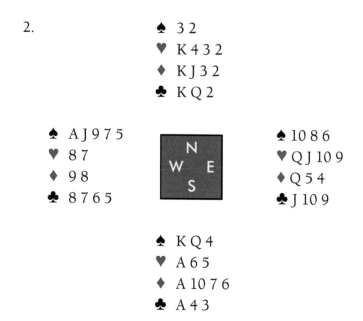

```
                    ♠ 3 2
                    ♥ K 4 3 2
                    ♦ K J 3 2
                    ♣ K Q 2

 ♠ A J 9 7 5          N          ♠ 10 8 6
 ♥ 8 7            W       E       ♥ Q J 10 9
 ♦ 9 8               S           ♦ Q 5 4
 ♣ 8 7 6 5                       ♣ J 10 9

                    ♠ K Q 4
                    ♥ A 6 5
                    ♦ A 10 7 6
                    ♣ A 4 3
```

SUGGESTED BIDDING: South deals and opens 1NT. The auction will proceed exactly as in hand #1.

OPENING LEAD: ♠7

THE PLAY: Declarer wins the first trick, noting that West has led from a suit headed by the ace and retains a tenace holding behind him (as in the first hand). He needs only three diamond tricks to make his contract, and should finesse in diamonds *through East*. If declarer loses a diamond trick to the queen in West's hand, he is safe from a spade lead and has nine tricks to cash on regaining the lead.

3.

♠ 3 2
♥ K 3 2
♦ 4 3 2
♣ A Q J 8 7

♠ A Q 9 5 4
♥ 6 5
♦ Q 10
♣ 6 5 4 3

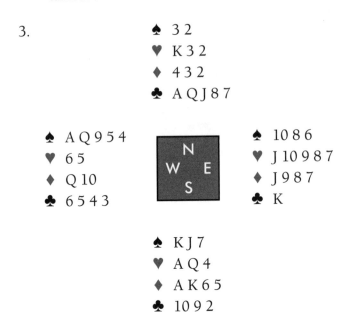

♠ 10 8 6
♥ J 10 9 8 7
♦ J 9 8 7
♣ K

♠ K J 7
♥ A Q 4
♦ A K 6 5
♣ 10 9 2

SUGGESTED BIDDING: South deals and opens 1NT, North raises to 3NT.

OPENING LEAD: ♠5

THE PLAY: Declarer wins the first trick. noting that West has led from a suit headed by the ace-queen. Trying hard to keep East from gaining the lead to play a spade through, declarer should lead a club to the *ace*. He is willing to let West win a club trick, but not East, so he guards against the singleton king in the East hand. (Note of interest: At matchpoint duplicate, declarer's best play would be the club finesse. Every pair holding these cards will play 3NT, so declarer cannot ignore a reasonable chance for two over-tricks to cater to such an unlikely holding as the singleton ♣K with East).

4.

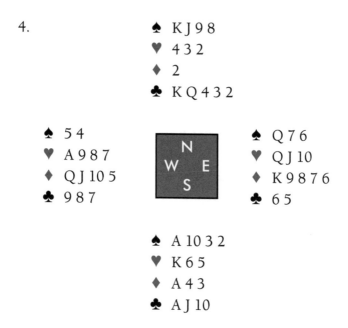

    ♠ K J 9 8
    ♥ 4 3 2
    ♦ 2
    ♣ K Q 4 3 2

♠ 5 4   ♠ Q 7 6
♥ A 9 8 7   ♥ Q J 10
♦ Q J 10 5   ♦ K 9 8 7 6
♣ 9 8 7   ♣ 6 5

    ♠ A 10 3 2
    ♥ K 6 5
    ♦ A 4 3
    ♣ A J 10

SUGGESTED BIDDING: South deals and opens 1NT. South responds 2♣ (Stayman). South rebids 2♠. North jumps to 4♠.

OPENING LEAD: ♦Q

THE PLAY: Declarer has plenty of winners. The danger is that he might lose a trump and three heart tricks. This can happen only if East wins a trump trick and leads a heart through declarer's king. So declarer should finesse in trumps *through East*. If he plays correctly, he will make 11 or 12 tricks.

Contract: 4♠ • Opening lead: K♦

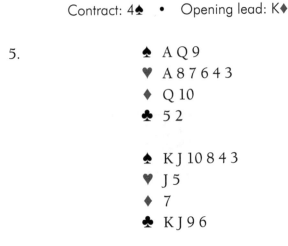

5.

♠ A Q 9
♥ A 8 7 6 4 3
♦ Q 10
♣ 5 2

♠ K J 10 8 4 3
♥ J 5
♦ 7
♣ K J 9 6

WEST	NORTH	EAST	SOUTH
1♦	1♥	2♦	2♠
3♦	3♠	Pass	4♠

All pass

West wins the first trick with the K♦ and then leads the A♦. How do you play so you lose only three tricks and make your contract?

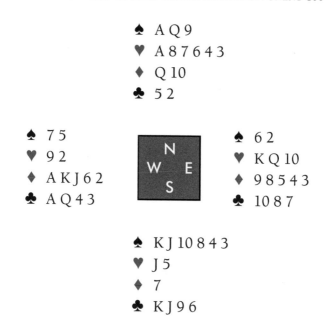

Answer: You should pitch a heart at trick two. Now you can set up dummy's hearts for three club discards, so you lose only two diamonds and one club. The only way to defeat 4♠ as the cards lie (with hearts splitting 3-2) is to lead a trump at trick two. Now you are an entry short to set up the hearts and reach them.

6.
          ♠ K 5 4
          ♥ Q 7
          ♦ 9 8 4 3
          ♣ A K 6 2

          ♠ A 9
          ♥ K 6 3
          ♦ A K 7 6 5
          ♣ 9 8 4

Contract: 3NT • Opening lead: 4♥

You win the first trick with the Q♥, so you know that West has the Ace. The K♥ is a stopper with West in the lead; if East obtains the lead, he can lead through your hearts to run the suit. If diamonds are 2-2 or if West has 3 diamonds, you can establish the suit without allowing East in the lead. When West has a singleton honor, you have to play very carefully.

At trick two, you lead a diamond from dummy and the defenders are helpless. When East plays the 2, you play a low card from your hand and West must win. If East plays the J or the Q at trick two, you can go back to dummy, finesse the other honor and pick up the entire suit without losing a trick). The other key play is the Q♥ from dummy at trick one or else you couldn't prevent the opponents from running the suit.

Look at the four hands:

6.

♠ K 5 4
♥ Q 7
♦ 9 8 4 3
♣ A K 6 2

♠ 8 7 3 2　　　　　　　　　　♠ Q J 10 6
♥ A J 9 4 2　　　♥ 10 8 5
♦ 10　　　　　　　　　　　　♦ Q J 2
♣ Q 10 5　　　　　　　　　　♣ J 7 3

♠ A 9
♥ K 6 3
♦ A K 7 6 5
♣ 9 8 4

NINETEEN

When a Contract Looks Difficult, Establish Your Side Suit Before Pulling Trump

"All things come round to him who will but wait."

—Henry Wadsworth Longfellow

I T IS OFTEN perfect strategy to pull trumps as soon as possible, to "get the children off the street," as they say. There are also many deals when it's best to delay playing the trump suit until your second suit is established.

When I was in Ireland last summer, my friend columnist Frank Stewart took a day off to kibitz the game in Belfast. Luckily, it was a session when an interesting column hand appeared.

The bidding certainly wasn't perfect, but it allowed us to share this fun board. It wasn't the greatest contract in the world and it's always good to get a little help from your friends.

West dealer • Neither side Vulnerable

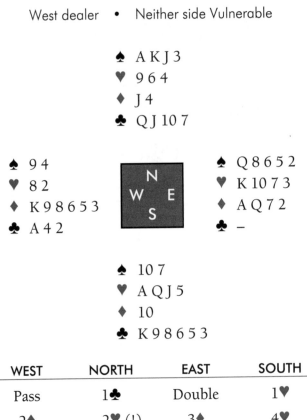

♠ A K J 3
♥ 9 6 4
♦ J 4
♣ Q J 10 7

♠ 9 4
♥ 8 2
♦ K 9 8 6 5 3
♣ A 4 2

♠ Q 8 6 5 2
♥ K 10 7 3
♦ A Q 7 2
♣ –

♠ 10 7
♥ A Q J 5
♦ 10
♣ K 9 8 6 5 3

WEST	NORTH	EAST	SOUTH
Pass	1♣	Double	1♥
2♦	2♥ (!)	3♦	4♥
All pass			

Opening lead: 6♦

I ruffed the second diamond and I was now down to three hearts in each hand. My best chance looked to be K-x-x of trumps in the East hand, so I crossed to dummy with the ♠A and led a trump to my jack.

Now it was time to turn my attention to the side suit, clubs, which I had to establish, because I was in danger of losing control in the trump suit.

West won the ♣A and made a crucial error by giving his partner a ruff. When East led a spade back to dummy, I pulled the outstanding trumps and claimed.

Even though trumps were 4-2, I succeeded because West gave his partner a ruff instead of continuing diamonds. West could have also continued a spade or East could have refused to ruff the club; either play would have doomed me to failure. Sometimes it's better to be fortunate than good.

Contract 4♥ • Opening lead: J ♠

♠ Q 6 5 4
♥ J 5
♦ 9 2
♣ Q 10 8 7 3

♠ 7
♥ A K Q 10 2
♦ A K Q 6 4
♣ 9 5

You are always going to lose at least one spade and two clubs, so you cannot afford any other losers. As long as the red suits don't split worse than 4-2, it is best to play AK of diamonds. Then ruff a low diamond with the ♥J. You can now pull trumps and claim because your diamonds are established.

Contract: 6♠ • Opening Lead: 9♣

♠ A 5 4 3
♥ 7
♦ 9 3
♣ A Q 8 7 4 2

♠ K Q J 10
♥ A K 10 8 5 2
♦ A
♣ 6 3

It appears that the opening lead is a singleton, so you take the ♣A. Now what is the best way to make 12 tricks?

Lead a heart to your ace and ruff a heart with a low spade. Return to your hand with a spade. Now ruff another heart with the ♠A, pull trump and claim. Here is the full hand:

♠ A 5 4 3
♥ 7
♦ 9 3
♣ A Q 8 7 4 2

♠ 7 6
♥ Q J 9 4
♦ K J 8 6 5 2
♣ 9

♠ 9 8 2
♥ 6 3
♦ Q J 10 7 4
♣ K J 10 5

♠ K Q J 10
♥ A K 10 8 5 2
♦ A
♣ 6 3

♠ K 10 4
♥ 6 5 4
♦ A 7
♣ A J 8 6 4

♠ A Q 5 3
♥ A 8 3
♦ 6 5 4
♣ K Q 7

You, South, opened 1♣ and partner responded 3♣. You tried 3♠ and partner raised to 4♠ (even though 3NT is cold). You decided you could handle a 4-3 fit and passed. The opening lead is the ♦Q. You win, fearing a heart switch. How should you continue?

You can make this contract if you can get all your club tricks. But if you draw three rounds of trumps and find a defender with a trump trick, he may ruff in before you can cash your clubs, leaving you stranded with losers. Note that you have ten winners even if you lose a trick in trumps. The solution, therefore, is to concede a trump trick early. Lead a trump from dummy and duck. You can win the return (if they lead diamonds, dummy can ruff), draw three more rounds of trumps, and run your clubs safely.

The last hand was more a matter of trump management than control.

During the session in Ireland that I refer to at the start of this principle, I opened one of my typical light opening bids. Frank Stewart, my kibitzer, would never have considered bidding with this hand. After a less-than-perfect result, I turned to him and agreed that I didn't quite have the proper values.

"I didn't have much of a hand, Frank."

Frank: "A hand? You didn't even have a foot!"

TWENTY

An Important Technique to Learn Is the Loser on Loser Play

"Timing in life is everything."

–John Sculley

THERE ARE MANY situations in bridge when losing a trick at the perfect time or to the correct opponent is the winning play. A loser on loser is playing a card that must be lost on a losing trick in another suit. I've included a few examples to help you recognize when these exciting opportunities appear.

This first hand is a classic loser on loser play from Alfred Sheinwold's "Puzzle Book #1," one of the first books I was privileged to edit and publish:

South dealer • All vulnerable • Opening lead: K♥

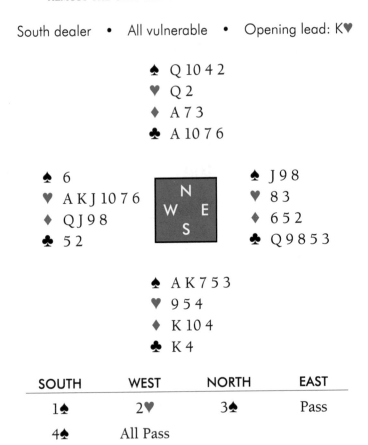

♠ Q 10 4 2
♥ Q 2
♦ A 7 3
♣ A 10 7 6

♠ 6
♥ A K J 10 7 6
♦ Q J 9 8
♣ 5 2

♠ J 9 8
♥ 8 3
♦ 6 5 2
♣ Q 9 8 5 3

♠ A K 7 5 3
♥ 9 5 4
♦ K 10 4
♣ K 4

SOUTH	WEST	NORTH	EAST
1♠	2♥	3♠	Pass
4♠	All Pass		

You are South, playing in 4♠. West cashes the ♥K and ♥A, as East plays the 8 and the 3. West continues with the ♥J. Many players would study the dummy, trying to decide whether to ruff with the queen or 10 of trumps. As you can plainly see, on this deal neither works; if you ruff with either card, you with lose four tricks and be defeated: two hearts, one trump trick and one diamond.

The key to this deal is simply pitching a diamond on the third round of hearts. This gives the defense three heart tricks, but then you lose no trump tricks and no diamonds (you can ruff the third diamond in dummy). You easily make your contract and partner can congratulate you on your winning play.

In the next deal, you can keep control by making a loser on loser play:

Timing the Ruff

A good 5-3 trump fit inspires confidence, but declarer may all too easily lose control if he allows his trumps to be shortened at an early stage in the play. Look at what happened on this hand.

Both Vulnerable • Dealer South

♠ Q 7 4
♥ 8 3
♦ K 7 6 2
♣ Q 10 8 5

♠ A K J 8 3
♥ 5
♦ A 9 4 3
♣ K J 2

SOUTH	WEST	NORTH	EAST
1♠	2♥	2♠	4♥
4♠	Pass	Pass	Pass

West led the queen of hearts to his partner's king and South ruffed the heart return. Game looked easy with five trumps, two diamonds and three clubs, but the snag became apparent when West discarded a club on the second round of trumps. If the remaining trumps were drawn, the defenders would be in a position to cash far too many hearts when in with the ace of clubs.

South tried to overcome the problem by switching to clubs after two rounds of trumps, but the defenders were not so obliging as to take the ace immediately. The king of clubs was allowed to win, but West took his ace of clubs on the second round and played a third club for his partner to ruff. South still had an unavoidable loser in diamonds and the contract went one down.

The complete deal:

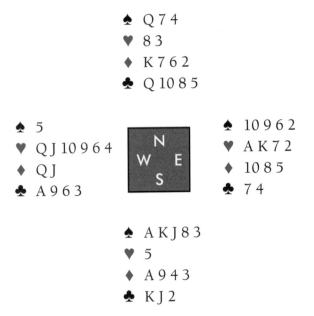

```
              ♠ Q 7 4
              ♥ 8 3
              ♦ K 7 6 2
              ♣ Q 10 8 5

♠ 5                         ♠ 10 9 6 2
♥ Q J 10 9 6 4    N         ♥ A K 7 2
♦ Q J           W   E       ♦ 10 8 5
♣ A 9 6 3         S         ♣ 7 4

              ♠ A K J 8 3
              ♥ 5
              ♦ A 9 4 3
              ♣ K J 2
```

Note the difference if South discards a diamond on the second heart instead of ruffing. This loser-on-loser play gives complete protection against the 4-1 trump break. If the defenders play a third heart the ruff can be taken in dummy, preserving South's trump holding intact. After drawing trumps, South can knock out the ace of clubs and claim the ten tricks that are rightfully his.

When you can afford it, discard a loser rather than allow your long trumps to be forced.

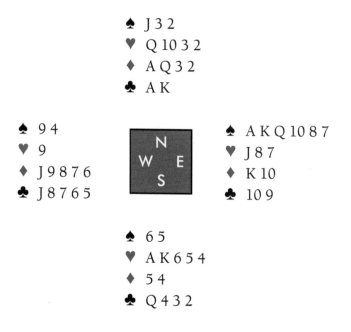

♠ J 3 2
♥ Q 10 3 2
♦ A Q 3 2
♣ A K

♠ 9 4
♥ 9
♦ J 9 8 7 6
♣ J 8 7 6 5

♠ A K Q 10 8 7
♥ J 8 7
♦ K 10
♣ 10 9

♠ 6 5
♥ A K 6 5 4
♦ 5 4
♣ Q 4 3 2

SUGGESTED BIDDING: East deals and opens 1♠. South and West pass and North reopens with a double. South responds 2♥. North raises to 3♥. South bids 4♥.

OPENING LEAD: ♠9

THE PLAY: Declarer should *pitch his losing diamond* on the third round of spades instead of ruffing low and risking an overruff or ruffing high at the risk of losing a trick to the ♥J. He can win any return, draw trumps, and make the rest easily. This is a *loser-on-loser play*.

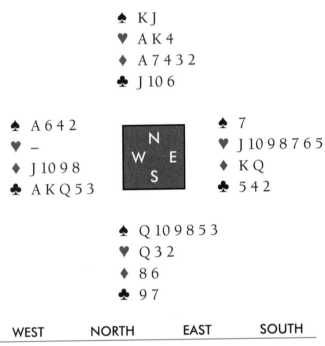

WEST	NORTH	EAST	SOUTH
		3♥	Pass
Pass	Double	Pass	3♠
All pass			

West leads three rounds of clubs. South sees that West is very likely void in hearts. South pitches his losing diamond on the third club, because he is concerned about a possible heart ruff to defeat the contract. If South had ruffed the third club, West can hold up until the second round when trumps are led, and shift to a diamond, ensuring a heart ruff because South cannot return to his hand without leading hearts or diamonds.

ALFRED (Freddie) SHEINWOLD (1912–1997). Alfred was one of the world's foremost bridge columnists, authors and analysts. He is best known for a brilliant writing career that spanned almost seven decades, and he was also an acclaimed champion player and international team captain. Sheinwold has many popular books; his most successful "Five Weeks to Winning Bridge" sold more than one million copies. He was editor of the *ACBL Bulletin*, as well as the most popular syndicated columnist in the world. Outside the bridge world, he was an expert singer. During World War II, he was the chief code and cipher expert of the Office of Strategic Services.

TWENTY-ONE

When You Need Another Trick as Declarer, Play All of Your Winners to Put Pressure on the Opponents

"Not knowing how near the truth is, we seek it far away."

—Hakruin

THIS IS SIMPLE ADVICE when you are in a notrump contract and you are a trick short of fulfilling it. If you have a long suit to run and don't have another reasonable method of winning that extra trick, go ahead and run that suit. You don't have to know intricate squeeze technique. Just go ahead and play out these winners and hope for an error by the opponents. Sometimes they have discarding problems and you never know when the extra trick will manifest itself for you.

♠ A K J 10 3
♥ Q 4
♦ K 9 8 5 2
♣ 7

♠ Q 5
♥ K J 9 6 2
♦ A 10
♣ Q 10 9 4

Both Vulnerable • Dealer West

WEST	NORTH	EAST	SOUTH
Pass	1♠	Pass	2♥
Pass	2♣	Pass	2NT
Pass	3♦	Pass	3NT
All pass			

This hand was played in a team game. Both tables reached 3NT and the declarers received the opening lead of the 3♣. At one table, East took the ♣K and ♣A and led a third round. Hoping that clubs were 4-4 or East had the ♥A, declarer played a low ♥ at trick four. West gratefully took his ace and cashed two more clubs tricks for down one.

After winning the ♣Q, the other declarer ran his five spades, discarding the ten of clubs and two hearts from his hand. West discarded three hearts, but then he had a real problem. If he pitched a club, declarer could simply knock out the ace of hearts, so he threw a diamond, hoping partner had the ten. Declarer's diamond suit was now good, so he gladly took 11 tricks when he had started with eight. This earned 12 IMPs for his side.

Here was the full hand:

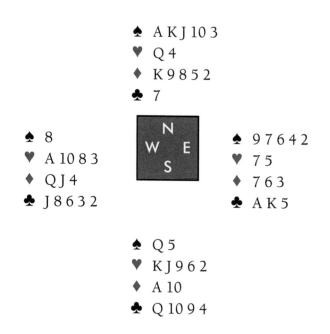

♠ A K J 10 3
♥ Q 4
♦ K 9 8 5 2
♣ 7

♠ 8
♥ A 10 8 3
♦ Q J 4
♣ J 8 6 3 2

♠ 9 7 6 4 2
♥ 7 5
♦ 7 6 3
♣ A K 5

♠ Q 5
♥ K J 9 6 2
♦ A 10
♣ Q 10 9 4

♠ ♡ ◇ ♣

TWENTY-TWO

Intermediate Cards Are Also Valuable

BY SHARON AUSTIN

"You need to let the little things that would usually bore you suddenly thrill you."

—Andy Warhol

WHEN EVALUATING your hand, remember intermediate cards (Pushers = 10s, 9s and 8s) backing up your face cards become as valuable as A-Q-J or K-J-7 when you are finessing as declarer. When you can finesse in a suit more than one time, they will frequently produce an extra trick.

EXAMPLE 1: With A-Q-2 opposite 6-5-3 you can lead toward the honors one time for a 50% chance of taking a trick with the queen, but when you have 10-9-8 instead of 6-5-3, your odds increase to 75% for two tricks (assuming you can lead again from that hand).

EXAMPLE 2: K-10-9-6 opposite A-3-2. You lead the ace and then the 2 to the 9, expecting to lose a trick (unless an

113

honor fell at the first trick). When we then play the 3 to the 10, this combination will produce 3 tricks at least 75% of the time because of our pushers.

EXAMPLE 3: K-10-9-6 opposite 5-3-2. Look how much better our chance is for an extra trick when we have the 10 and 9 instead of two low cards along with the king.

Pushers are a great addition to any hand. When you are evaluating your hand after partner opens a 15–17 1NT, you can add another point when holding K-10-9-7 in a suit. You should also consider these intermediate cards when partner opens a suit and you have a fit with him.

On defense, pushers are important on opening leads. They form helpful sequences such as Q-J-10-3, Q-J-9-3, A-10-9-6, K-10-9-5, Q-10-9-4, 10-9-8-2 and 10-9-7-6.

They are also useful in the middle of a deal to make a surround play on defense such as the following example:

Dummy has 10-8-4 and you hold K-J-9-2. When you are on lead what do you play? The J is the proper card to surround the declarer's queen if your partner has the ace. It also works well if partner has the queen and declarer the ace.

Always remember to look for your pushers!

SHARON AUSTIN started playing bridge in Junior High School and continued after her marriage. She has two daughters. Sharon became a Life Master in three years and then was elected president of her unit in Indianapolis. She is currently manager of the Indianapolis Bridge Center and one of the top teachers in the Midwest.

♠ ♡ ◇ ♣

TWENTY-THREE

No Five Card Suit in Dummy Should Ever Be Ignored

BY MARTI RONEMUS

"It takes extraordinary intelligence to contemplate the obvious."

—Alfred North Whitehead

OFTEN WHEN WE'RE in trouble with too many darn losers and we can't _trump_ losers in dummy, we can _dump_ losers by establishing a long suit in dummy. The key is either protecting or creating entries. This should be the heart (pun intended) of our plan. When evaluating our hand as responder, we shouldn't undervalue that five-carder, no matter how ratty. Let's work on this skill.

Here are two hands, illustrating the power of that five-card suit.

#1 • ♠A lead

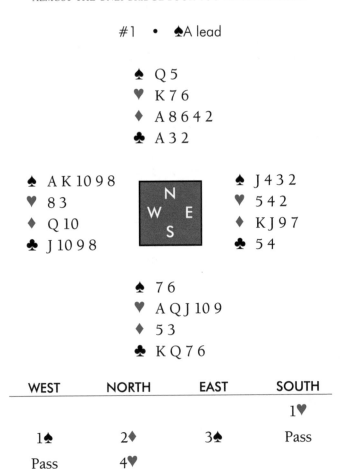

♠ Q 5
♥ K 7 6
♦ A 8 6 4 2
♣ A 3 2

♠ A K 10 9 8
♥ 8 3
♦ Q 10
♣ J 10 9 8

♠ J 4 3 2
♥ 5 4 2
♦ K J 9 7
♣ 5 4

♠ 7 6
♥ A Q J 10 9
♦ 5 3
♣ K Q 7 6

WEST	NORTH	EAST	SOUTH
			1♥
1♠	2♦	3♠	Pass
Pass	4♥		

BIDDING: North knows when Pard opens that the pair will be in Hearts, and at least in game. After East's 2♠ bid, with our minimum hand, we elect to Pass, leaving it up to Pard.

PLAY: losers: we have 2 Spades, 0 Hearts, and 1 Diamond. We are aware of the 4th round Club, which is very likely a loser also. BUT!! Look at the Diamonds in dummy. We

116

lose tricks 1 and 2. At trick 3, West smartly switches to the ♣J which we win in hand, so we can preserve an entry. Next, the key move: we play a Diamond and _duck_! We win the return (probably a Club), play to our ♦A and ruff (high) a Diamond.

Then we pull trump, ending in dummy. We then play and ruff the 4th round of Diamonds. Finally, back to dummy with our ♣A, Dummy's lovely five-carder saves the day.

Our next hand isn't quite as easy.

#2 • ♦J lead

```
                ♠ J 9 6 5 3
                ♥ K Q
                ♦ K 4 2
                ♣ A J 6

   ♠ A 10 8 7          N          ♠ K Q 4
   ♥ 7 2          W         E     ♥ 9 5 3
   ♦ J 10 9 3          S          ♦ Q 8 6
   ♣ Q 7 5                        ♣ K 9 8 4

                ♠ 2
                ♥ A J 10 8 6 4
                ♦ A 7 5
                ♣ 10 3 2
```

WEST	NORTH	EAST	SOUTH
			2♥
Pass	2NT	Pass	3♦
Pass	4♥		

BIDDING: Pard's 2NT bid is asking us if we have an Ace or King outside our Big Suit. We do. And that's all Pard needs to know to go to game.

PLAY: We have 1 Spade loser, 1 Diamond and likely 2 Clubs. Can we pull the fat out of the fire by developing that five-card Spade suit? The Spades are quite a challenge, but what fun!

We take trick 1 in hand with the ♦A and immediately give up a Spade. We win the return (which should be a Diamond...foolish for East to lead anything else) and at trick 4 while in dummy, lead one of dummy's Spades, which we ruff high in hand. Then, a trump back up to dummy and ruff a Spade. Back to dummy with another Heart and ruff another Spade. Pull the last trump, and return to dummy with a Club. We can discard any loser on the winning fifth Spade and concede the last two tricks.

Imagine turning that ratty suit into such a winner. Our opponents and Pard are amazed.

MARTI RONEMUS, with husband Gary, owned and ran one of Pennsylvania's three biggest bridge clubs for 15 years. She has written over 100 articles for the *Bridge Bulletin* and *Daily Bulletin*, managed the *Easybridge!* program, and currently writes over 18 columns a month for *Vu-Bridge*. To find out more about her Bridge Boot Camp vacations, reach out to mronemus@comcast.net. Her popular *Bidding Flash Cards* are available from baronbarclay.com.

SECTION THREE

Defense

♠ ♡ ◇ ♣

TWENTY-FOUR

Study the Six Types of Defenses Against Suit Contracts

"Everything is complicated if no one explains it to you."

—Fredrik Backman

MOST OF THE TIME, you'll have clues from the bidding to help you and your partner decide which kind of defense is the most likely to succeed. It's crucial to sort through this information, so the opening lead will start you on the right path.

The more experience you have, the more you'll be able to calculate your best chance for winning defense. Frequently, you'll have to switch plans during the play; sometimes you might switch several times, depending on the dummy, the bidding and how declarer plays from trick to trick.

Here are the six main defenses to suit contracts. One of the important qualities of a top defender is knowing when he should strive to take tricks quickly and when he can relax and wait patiently for the tricks to come to him.

When the defenders see dummy, they must assess its strengths, discern what source of tricks it will provide declarer, and imagine how declarer will conduct the play (and how much success he will have). Depending on dummy's assets, the defenders' approach will vary. We will look at six possible defensive strategies against a suit contract. (Only rarely will the right approach fall into no particular category.) Of the six, the first two are the most important.

    I. **ACTIVE.** Suppose you defend 4♠, and dummy is:

        ♠ A Q x
        ♥ x x x
        ♦ x
        ♣ K Q J 10 x x

    How will declarer use this dummy? What tricks will it supply? It's clear what will happen. Declarer will set up the clubs (if he doesn't already hold the ace) and have plenty of discards for his losers. If you face this imposing dummy, you have no choice — you must get busy, going after your tricks before declarer draws trumps and uses the clubs. A heart lead is mandatory. Laying down the ♥A from A-Q-x or leading from the king or queen is justified. Even if the worst happens, and you lead into the jaws of declarer's A-Q or A-K-J, you lose nothing. Declarer would have thrown his losers on the clubs anyhow. Also, if you hold the ♦A, you'll cash it before it goes away.

Let's put this concept into a full deal:

1.

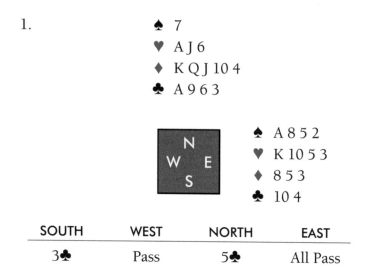

	♠ 7
	♥ A J 6
	♦ K Q J 10 4
	♣ A 9 6 3

♠ A 8 5 2
♥ K 10 5 3
♦ 8 5 3
♣ 10 4

SOUTH	WEST	NORTH	EAST
3♣	Pass	5♣	All Pass

South's 3♣ opening is preemptive, suggesting seven good clubs and little else, and is intended to interfere with your bidding. This time, however, North has a good hand and raises to game. West leads the ♠Q, and you take your ace. **What do you lead at trick two?**

Your partner will have the ♦A, since South would be too strong to preempt with the ♠K and ♦A plus his seven good clubs. So the setting trick must come from hearts. *With dummy's diamond staring you in the face, it's time to get busy.* Shift to a low heart hoping partner has the queen. Perhaps you can set up a heart trick before declarer sets up the diamonds and throws his heart losers away,

2.

♠ J 7 5
♥ 9 6 4
♦ Q 5
♣ A K Q 10 6

♠ 9 6 4
♥ A K 10 5 2
♦ K 6 2
♣ J 9

SOUTH	WEST	NORTH	EAST
1♠	Pass	2♣	Pass
2♠	Pass	4♠	All Pass

You cash your top hearts against the 4♠ contract, declarer dropping the jack and queen. **What do you do next?**

Again, declarer has the tricks to make his contract unless the defenders take their tricks first. Lead a low diamond, hoping partner has the ace and declarer's hand is something like:

♠ A K Q x x x
♥ Q J
♦ J x x
♣ x x

You won't beat this contract if declarer has the ♦A. If partner has it, you must cash your diamond tricks without delay, since *dummy's clubs will provide discards.*

124

II. PASSIVE. Note well: players often mishandle this type of defense. Failure to understand the active-vs.-passive concept is one of the most common defensive errors.

If you are defending 4♠ again, but this time dummy is:

      ♠ Q 6 5
      ♥ 8 6 4
      ♦ J 7 5
      ♣ 9 7 6 3

A sterile dummy is a common sight. What tricks will this dummy provide? Right, not much. Dummy has no high-card tricks, no long suit to set up, no ruffing power. When declarer must struggle with a weak dummy, *his losers are unavoidable.* Since declarer can't get rid of his losers, the defenders should *wait* for the tricks they are bound to get sooner or later. Nothing dynamic is required; *aggressive play is avoided.*

This dummy calls for a PASSIVE defense. The passive approach is the antithesis of the busy approach. If you find yourself on lead, try to *exit safely.* Don't take chances and give declarer tricks that aren't his for the taking. A trump lead may be safe — that's probably declarer's strongest suit. A lead from a sequence is safe enough. If declarer leads a suit and you win a trick in it (perhaps after declarer loses a finesse), you might lead the same suit right back; when declarer breaks a suit, to lead it becomes less dangerous.

Another safe way to exit is to lead something that declarer must ruff with a long trump. His trumps will be winners anyway, so you don't mind if he ruffs with one of them.

What you must avoid in a passive defense, however, is getting busy — laying down aces, leading from honors, breaking new suits. You may give declarer a free finesse that he lacks the entries to take, let him avoid a finesse that would have lost, establish intermediate cards for him, eliminate his guesswork and generally make the play easier for him.

3.

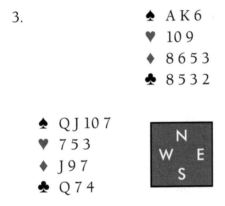

♠ A K 6
♥ 10 9
♦ 8 6 5 3
♣ 8 5 3 2

♠ Q J 10 7
♥ 7 5 3
♦ J 9 7
♣ Q 7 4

SOUTH	WEST	NORTH	EAST
1♥	Pass	1NT	Pass
4♥	All pass		

You lead the ♠Q. Declarer takes the top spades in dummy, discarding a low diamond on the second round, and leads a club to his jack and your queen. **What do you lead at this point?**

What is dummy like? Zilch. **Must the defenders hurry to win minor-suit tricks?** No. If declarer has club or diamond losers, he can't get rid of them. **What type of**

defense does this suggest? Passive. **What is a safe exit for West at this point?** He should lead a high spade and force declarer to spend a trump. Any other lead may *help declarer*. Declarer's hand could be:

♠ x
♥ A K Q x x x
♦ A Q x
♣ A J 10

A club or diamond return gives him a free finesse, and a heart gives him a dummy entry to take a minor-suit finesse.

4.

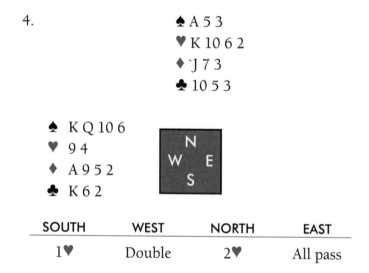

SOUTH	WEST	NORTH	EAST
1♥	Double	2♥	All pass

You lead the ♠K. Declarer wins the ace, draws two rounds of trumps, ending in dummy (East follows), and leads a diamond to his king and your ace. **What do you lead now?**

Since dummy is flat and weak, you should stay *passive*. Just return a diamond. Declarer plays the jack from dummy and Partner wins the queen. A spade is returned, and you win the 10 and queen, partner and declarer both following. **What next?**

The dummy is *still* flat and weak, so you don't need to look for club tricks. Lead another diamond instead. Partner plays the 10, and declarer ruffs. Declarer then leads a trump to dummy and a club to his jack. You win your king. *Return a passive club.* Partner plays the 9. Declarer wins the ace, but must lose another club to partner's queen in the end. The contract is down one. The full deal:

```
              ♠ A 5 3
              ♥ K 10 6 2
              ♦ J 7 3
              ♣ 10 5 3

   ♠ K Q 10 6      N         ♠ 9 4 2
   ♥ 9 4       W     E       ♥ 8 7
   ♦ A 9 5 2       S         ♦ Q 10 8 4
   ♣ K 6 2                   ♣ Q 9 8 4

              ♠ J 8 7
              ♥ A Q J 5 3
              ♦ K 6
              ♣ A J 7
```

This is a perfect passive defense. The defenders got out of the lead *safely* every time: (Declarer can do better by forcing the defenders to help him. He can, for instance, lead a spade from dummy after drawing trumps. West wins two spade tricks but then must break a minor suit or give declarer a ruff-and-discard with a spade lead).

Of course, at times you won't be sure whether to get active or go passive. The old standby of counting declarer's tricks may help by telling you whether you need your tricks in a hurry.

Several other strategies are available to the defenders. For example...

III. LEADING TRUMPS. Suppose the contract is the usual 4♠, and dummy is:

♠ Q x x
♥ x
♦ x x x x x
♣ J x x

What source of tricks does this dummy contain? Obviously, declarer can use this dummy only for ruffing tricks. If he has losing hearts, he will try to ruff them. The defenders should lead trumps, hoping to strand declarer with his losers. Drawing two of declarer's trumps for the price of one is the right approach when declarer can take extra tricks by using his trumps separately .

5.

♠ 8
♥ Q 7 5
♦ K 6 5 4
♣ J 7 5 4 2

♠ J 5
♥ 9 6 4
♦ Q 10 9 8
♣ A K 10 6

```
    N
W       E
    S
```

SOUTH	WEST	NORTH	EAST
1♠	Pass	1NT	Pass
2♥	All pass		

You lead the ♣A, winning the first trick. What next?

Dummy's ♦K may be a trick, but you can't help that. However, declarer will probably want to ruff spades in dummy (in fact, declarer may play the entire hand as a crossruff if he is short in clubs) and you can reduce dummy's ruffing power. Shift to a trump at trick two.

Note that your partner probably has five spades, so declarer may well have losing spades to ruff. And dummy has no other source of tricks for you to worry about. (You might have led a trump at trick one, anticipating the dummy from the bidding).

Now for some rare strategies vs. suit contracts:

IV. FORCING DEFENSE.
In a forcing defense, you make declarer lose control of the play by forcing him to ruff so many times that he runs out of trumps! This approach

is attractive when a defender has unexpected length in trumps — usually four cards or more.

To force declarer, you usually start by leading your longest suit. Maybe declarer is short there and will soon have to ruff. In this deal your long suit is strong, increasing your chance of success.

6.

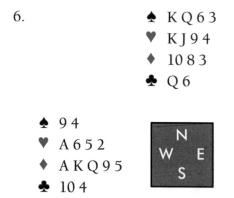

♠	K Q 6 3
♥	K J 9 4
♦	10 8 3
♣	Q 6

♠ 9 4
♥ A 6 5 2
♦ A K Q 9 5
♣ 10 4

SOUTH	WEST	NORTH	EAST
1NT	2♦	3♦	Pass
3♥	Pass	4♥	All pass

North's 3♦ cuebid was a form of the *Stayman convention*. You lead three top diamonds, and declarer ruffs the third round. Declarer next leads a trump. **How do you plan the defense?**

You know declarer is playing a 4-4 trump fit, and your four trumps may be a nuisance. You already forced declarer to ruff in his hand, so if you can shorten *dummy*, declarer will be out of control — you'll have more trumps than he has in either hand.

To force dummy, you must wait until declarer is out of trumps in his hand. Therefore, when declarer leads a trump to the king and a trump back to his queen, you must duck both times. (If you mistakenly win and lead another diamond, declarer can ruff in his hand, preserving dummy's trump length and keeping control). If declarer leads a third trump, you win, and now a diamond lead accomplishes your goal by forcing dummy to ruff. You'll be left in control with your last trump.

(A good declarer will abandon trumps after he sees the 4-1 trump break. He will lead black-suit winners, letting West score a low heart for down one, but keeping control and avoiding down two).

Conceding a *ruff-and-discard* can cost the defense a trick, but if declarer has no losers that a ruff-and-discard will let him avoid, it may be an effective way to attack his trump holding. In the problem above, if dummy were:

♠ K Q 6 3
♥ K J 9 4
♦ 10 8
♣ Q 6 2

West should still lead three rounds of diamonds, even if declarer gets a ruff-and-discard. On the bidding, declarer has all the missing high cards, so a ruff-and-discard can't help him and may weaken his trumps.

One word of caution. Occasionally, a persistent forcing defense may help declarer by letting him score several low trumps that otherwise would not win tricks. The objective of a forcing defense is to make it impossible for declarer to draw trumps so he can't use his side suits. Beware of a forcing defense if your trump holding is very long *and strong*, or if declarer has fast side-suit tricks he can cash without drawing trumps.

V. **TRYING FOR RUFFS.** Like many players, you may be fond of this approach. If you have a side-suit singleton, it hits the table at almost the speed of light. You just know partner will produce the ace and return the suit for you to ruff. You like leading doubletons almost as much. Perhaps, then, we should emphasize when you shouldn't try for a ruff by leading from shortness.

1. When you have natural trump tricks.
2. When you have great length in trumps. Even if a ruff is available, a forcing defense may work better. (Rare exception: Try for ruffs when you fear that declarer may be able to endplay you in trumps).
3. When you have a strong hand. If partner's hand is weak, he may never get in to give you your ruff.
4. When declarer can probably draw trumps before you get a ruff. (However, if you hold the trump ace or king — a fast reentry — your chances of getting a ruff are much better).
5. When the contract will be defeated anyway if partner has a trick. Look at this situation:

You, West, hold:

7.
        ♠ 10 7 5 3
        ♥ A K 4
        ♦ 9 7 5 4 2
        ♣ 4

SOUTH	WEST	NORTH	EAST
		1♣	Pass
1♥	Pass	2♥	Pass
3♣	Pass	4♥	Pass
5♥	All Pass		

What is your lead?

To lead your singleton club would be misguided. If partner has the ♣A, the contract will always fail. But partner is much more likely, on this bidding, to hold Q-x-x or J-10-x-x, in which case a club lead may pick up his holding for declarer.

A *risk* always goes with leading from shortness. Your short suit may be the opponents' long suit — a suit they will use for tricks. Leading the suit may help them establish it. Therefore, risk a short-suit lead only when conditions look right.

VI. EXTRA TRUMP TRICKS. It's often hard to imagine winning tricks in the opponents' best suit. Nevertheless, an UPPERCUT or TRUMP PROMOTION may be your only chance to defeat the contract.

In an uppercut a defender ruffs with an intermediate card, forcing declarer to weaken his trumps by spending a high trump to overruff.

8.

♠ A K 6 3
♥ 5
♦ 9 6 2
♣ A K Q 7 3

♠ 10 5
♥ A 9 2
♦ K Q 10 8 5 3
♣ 9 4

SOUTH	WEST	NORTH	EAST
2♥ (1)	Pass	2NT	Pass
3♥ (2)	Pass	4♥	All pass

(1) Weak two-bid
(2) No side ace or king

You lead the ♦K. Partner overtakes and returns a diamond. Declarer follows with the jack the second time. **How do you defend?**

No more side-suit tricks are available, so the trump suit offers the only chance for a fourth trick. At trick three lead a low diamond, forcing partner to ruff. He ruffs with the ♥7, and declarer overruffs with the 10. Your ♥9 begins to look better. When declarer leads the ♥K, you grab your ace and lead a fourth diamond. This time partner ruffs with the 8. When declarer must overruff with another honor, your 9 is suddenly worth a trick! The other hands are:

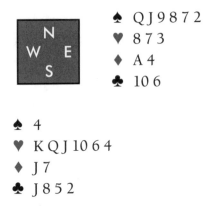

- ♠ Q J 9 8 7 2
- ♥ 8 7 3
- ♦ A 4
- ♣ 10 6

♠ 4
♥ K Q J 10 6 4
♦ J 7
♣ J 8 5 2

An important part of this strategy is that the defense must cash their side winners before attacking declarer's trump holding; otherwise, declarer may survive with a loser-on-loser play.

In the last deal, if West had the ♠A instead of dummy, he would need to cash it before leading a third round of diamonds. If he did not, declarer would discard his losing spade instead of overruffing East at the cost of a trump honor.

The position below illustrates a TRUMP PROMOTION.

♥ 3 2

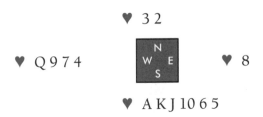

♥ Q 9 7 4   ♥ 8

♥ A K J 10 6 5

Hearts are trumps. East leads a diamond, in which both West and declarer are void. Declarer ruffs with the ♥J. West should decline to overruff, and now his trump holding is worth two tricks. (It is seldom right to overruff with a natural trump winner, as the ♥Q is here. If you save your trumps, their value may increase).

Let's review the six types of defenses to suit contracts. Remember, above all, that a good defender knows when he must take tricks in a hurry and when he can wait patiently for his tricks.

1. ACTIVE, indicated if dummy (or perhaps declarer) has a long, strong side suit that will provide discards.
2. PASSIVE, indicated if dummy lacks trick-taking power and declarer will have trouble avoiding losers.
3. TRUMP LEADS, indicated if dummy's only source of tricks is ruffing power.
4. FORCING, in which the defenders make declarer ruff so many times that he runs out of trumps and can't use his side suits. This defense is attractive when a defender has extra length in trumps.
5. TRYING FOR RUFFS, best when (1) you have trump control, and (2) your partner has an entry to give you a ruff.
6. EXTRA TRUMP TRICKS. In an uppercut, a defender ruffs with an intermediate trump, forcing declarer to weaken his trump holding by overruffing. In a trump promotion, declarer must either ruff low and be overruffed or ruff high at the cost of strengthening a defender's trump holding. Winning unexpected trump tricks may be the defenders' only chance.

TWENTY-FIVE

Good Defense Is Often Knowing Whether to Be Active or Passive Against a Suit Contract

"What we have here is a failure to communicate."

—From "Cool Hand Luke"

T HE FAILURE to understand this concept is one of the most common defensive errors. There are distinct differences between these two types of defenses which we discussed briefly in Principle #24.

- ACTIVE: This is indicated when the defense needs to get busy because the dummy or declarer possesses a long, strong side suit that will provide discards. In this situation, the defense must try to take tricks quickly. They will make aggressive, risky plays such as cashing aces, and leading from kings and queens in a desperate attempt to establish and cash fast tricks before declarer can use his assets.

- **PASSIVE:** This is indicated when dummy lacks trick-taking power and the declarer will have trouble avoiding losers. In such a case, the defenders' goal is to exit safely whenever either finds himself on lead. They are trying not to give away tricks that the declarer cannot take or develop on his own.

There are many card combinations called "frozen suits" that will cost the declarer or the defenders a trick if their side leads or "breaks" the suit first. It's important to avoid leading these suits whenever possible.

Quiz On Strategy vs. Suit Contracts

1.
        ♠ K 10 3 2
        ♥ A 7 5
        ♦ Q 8 4
        ♣ A J 3

♠ Q 7 5
♥ K Q J 2
♦ K 9 3
♣ 8 6 4

You are defending 2♠. North opened 1♣, South bid 1♠, North raised. Declarer wins your ♥K with the ace and leads the ♠K and a spade to the jack. You win the queen and cash the ♥Q and ♥J, all following. How do you continue?

2.

    ♠ A Q
    ♥ J 9 6 4
    ♦ A J 3
    ♣ K 7 5 2

♠ 8 4
♥ K Q 5
♦ K 10 5 2
♣ Q J 10 8

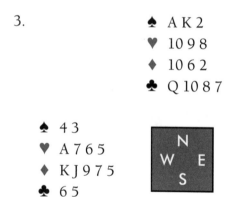

You defend 4♥. Dummy opened 1NT, declarer responded 3♠ and converted 3NT to 4♥. Your ♣Q holds the first trick, but declarer ruffs the next club. He leads a spade to the ace and finesses the ♥J to your queen . What do you lead?

3.

    ♠ A K 2
    ♥ 10 9 8
    ♦ 10 6 2
    ♣ Q 10 8 7

♠ 4 3
♥ A 7 6 5
♦ K J 9 7 5
♣ 6 5

You defend 4♥. Declarer opened 1♥, dummy raised and declarer went on to game. You lead a diamond to partner's ace. He cashes the ♦Q and leads a third diamond, ruffed by declarer . Declarer now leads the ♥K. How do you defend?

4.

♠ A Q 4
♥ 7 6
♦ 8 7 6
♣ A Q J 10 5

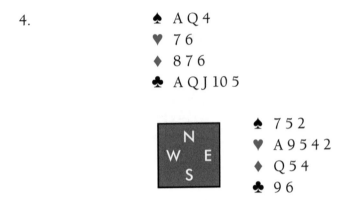

♠ 7 5 2
♥ A 9 5 4 2
♦ Q 5 4
♣ 9 6

You defend 4♠. Declarer opened 1♠, dummy responded 2♣ and raised declarer's 2♠ rebid to game. Partner leads the ♥Q. How do you defend?

5.

♠ 7 6 3 2
♥ A J 3 2
♦ 3
♣ 10 9 8 7

♠ K Q 10 5
♥ Q 10 9 8
♦ Q 9
♣ 6 5 4

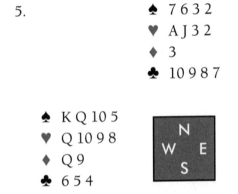

You defend 2♣. Declarer opened 1♦, dummy responded 1♥ and passed declarer's 2♣ rebid. Your ♠K holds the first trick, partner playing the 9 and declarer the jack. What do you do now?

6.
      ♠ A K 3
      ♥ 3
      ♦ J 7 6 5
      ♣ A Q 6 5 4

♠ 6 5 4
♥ A 9 2
♦ 9 8
♣ 10 8 7 3 2

You defend 4♥. Your partner opened 1♦, and declarer preempted with 4♥. Partner overtakes your ♦9 lead with the 10 and cashes the queen. On the ♦K, declarer ruffs with the ♥K. How do you defend?

7.
      ♠ 9 5 4
      ♥ J 8 6
      ♦ A K Q 10 4
      ♣ Q 7

♠ A K 10 6 3
♥ 9 5 2
♦ J 9
♣ K 8 2

You defend 4♥. Declarer opened 1♥, you overcalled 1♠. Dummy bid 2♦ and raised declarer's 2♥ rebid to game. You cash the ♠A and ♠K, declarer following with the jack and queen. What do you lead at trick three?

8. You, West, hold:

♠ A Q 7 5 3
♥ A K 5
♦ 10 9 7 4
♣ 2

SOUTH	WEST	NORTH	EAST
1♥	1♠	2♣	Pass
3♣	Pass	3♥	Pass
4♥	All Pass		

What is your opening lead?

SOLUTIONS

1. Go passive by returning your last trump. With dummy so weak, your minor-suit tricks aren't going anywhere. Let declarer break the minor suits.
2. Get active with a diamond return, hoping to set up a trick if partner has the queen. If you don't lead a diamond now, declarer will have time to draw trumps and discard dummy's diamonds on his spades. If he has a losing diamond, he will then ruff it in dummy.
3. Hold up your ace of trumps until dummy has none left. Then you can force declarer to ruff another diamond lead in his hand. If he started with only five trumps, he will lose control — you will have a long trump and a good diamond. If declarer stops playing trumps after seeing the 4-1 split, he can keep control

by cashing his black-suit winners and forcing you to ruff with your low trump. Nevertheless, you get four tricks.

4. Win the ♥A and shift to the ♦Q. You need three fast diamond tricks to beat the contract, and partner must therefore hold A-J-10. If you lead a low diamond instead, declarer will play low, ducking the trick safely to partner and losing only two diamonds.

5. Shift to trumps to cut down on dummy's only source of tricks. (You also keep declarer from ruffing spades in his hand).

6. You should discard on the third diamond. If partner has a trump as high as the 10, your A-9-2 will then be worth two tricks. If you overruff the ♥K with your ace, you are letting declarer force out your ace with his king, which he intended to do anyway. It is seldom right to overruff with a natural trump winner. Let your trumps increase in value.

7. Shift to a club, hoping declarer's hand is something like:

> ♠ Q J
> ♥ A K Q x x x
> ♦ x x
> ♣ J x x

You can't beat the contract if declarer holds the ♣A.

8. Lead the ♦10. Avoid leading your club singleton, since the contract will always be defeated if partner has the ♣A. If, as is far more likely, he has the ♣Q or ♣J, a club lead will help declarer.

TWENTY-SIX

Avoid These Six Dangerous Leads
BY EASLEY BLACKWOOD

"There is safety in the very heart of danger."

–Vincent van Gogh

1. The lead of an unsupported ace in an unbid suit (Also see Principle #28).

There are times when you will have dangerous holdings in each of the four suits, and you are just going to have to choose the one which you consider the least dangerous. They tell a story of a famous player who told a pupil of his never to lead from a suit headed by a jack. One day, the pupil looked at his hand, and quit the game forever. All four of his suits were headed by jacks. Better he should have reviewed the bidding to determine which suit would be the least dangerous, or possibly to get a clue that one of them was not likely to be dangerous at all. I am going to start with those leads which seem least bad, and work up to the ones which I consider the worst of all.

What do you lead from the West hand against a 4♠ contract when South had opened the bidding with 1♠ and North has gone straight to four?

```
                    ♠ K 9 8 4 3 2
                    ♥ 10 5
                    ♦ 8 6
                    ♣ K Q 2

  ♠ Q 7                N            ♠ —
  ♥ A 9            W       E        ♥ Q J 8 4 3 2
  ♦ A J 5 3 2          S            ♦ K Q 9 4
  ♣ 9 6 4 3                         ♣ 10 8 5

                    ♠ A J 10 6 5
                    ♥ K 7 6
                    ♦ 10 7
                    ♣ A J 7
```

The hand is from the Great Britain vs. North America match from the 1962 World Championship. The bidding was the same in both rooms. Terence Reese, West for Great Britain, led the ace of hearts. Robert Nail, for North America, led the three of clubs. In this instance, Nail turned out to be right, and Reese turned out to be wrong.

Now let's see what merit we can find in the lead of a club. From Nail's viewpoint, why lead either ace? He held eleven HCPs himself, and this made it almost a certainty that South held more HCPs than did East. There was nothing in the bidding to indicate that anybody had any long side suits on which losers could be discarded. It seemed better to make a passive lead and just lie back and let declarer lead those red suits up to his hand. Against the passive club lead, Claude Rodrigue, South for Great Britain, didn't have a chance. He won his ace, drew trumps, cashed dummy's two clubs, and led a diamond. East rose with the queen, and led the queen of hearts. The defense now took two heart tricks and another diamond trick for down one.

Leading unsupported aces does not constitute a good opening lead, but at times when all other leads are worse, that may be the lead you will choose.

2. The blind lead of a short suit, a singleton or doubleton.

One of the objections to this lead is that it often helps the declarer establish his secondary suit. I spent some time looking for the worst example of this I could find from actual play, and while I had to go all the way to Perth, Australia, I found one which will do. It was played in the fall of 1977, in the National Australian Championship.

E-W vulnerable • Dealer North

♠ A 10 6
♥ 8 7 5 4
♦ J 6 3
♣ J 3 2

♠ K Q J 9 5 4
♥ Q 9 6
♦ 10
♣ Q 8 5

N
W E
S

♠ 7 3 2
♥ 10
♦ K 9 7 4 2
♣ A 10 6 4

♠ 8
♥ A K J 3 2
♦ A Q 8 5
♣ K 9 7

SOUTH	WEST	NORTH	EAST
		Pass	Pass
1♥	1♠	2♥	2♠
4♥	All pass		

The opening lead in one room was the ten of diamonds. West's hand is an excellent example of when not to lead a singleton: he had a natural trump trick, but no useless trumps; thus, even if he does get his ruff, it is likely to cost him a trump trick. It is likely that the diamond suit is the opponent's second suit. The ten is a valuable enough card on its own — wasting it on the opening lead may enable the declarer to play the suit in such a way that he would be unlikely to find if left to his own devices.

When a defender has bid a suit, has been supported, and leads a different suit, the lead is likely to be a singleton. They know about that south of the equator just as well as we do up here in the Northern Hemisphere. South played the ten of diamonds to be a singleton. The ten was covered by the jack, king and ace. Declarer cashed the ace and king of trumps, played a spade to dummy's ace, and led a small diamond to the eight in his hand. West chose to discard a spade. Declarer led the queen of diamonds and West discarded a second spade, again refusing to trump. Declarer trumped his last diamond in dummy, ruffed a spade in his hand, and put West on lead by playing a heart. Now he was going to make his king of clubs no matter who had the ace. West was down to the singleton king of spades and three clubs. South discarded a club when West cashed the spade king. West had nothing left but clubs. A club to East's ace and a club return gave South his tenth trick. Altogether he lost one trick each in hearts, spades and clubs.

Try taking ten tricks with South hand against the lead of the king of spades.

3. The lead of a suit bid by the dummy.

When inexperienced players don't have a short suit to lead, they frequently lead the suit bid by the dummy, on the theory that they are "leading through strength". This maxim would be better if it read "lead through strength except when it is also length". Better still, there might be another maxim which says, "Stay away from long suits held by either declarer or dummy." This admonition applies particularly when the suits are five cards long or longer, as they well may be when the dummy has bid them. Unless there is something in the bidding to suggest otherwise, it is better to lead your suits than it is to lead declarer's suits. When you lead his suits, too often you are helping him get those suits established.

4. The lead of a doubleton queen or jack in a suit your partner has not bid.
5. The lead of a suit (not trumps) bid on your right.
6. The underlead of an ace against a suit contract (Also see Principle #27).

The late Joe Cain, of Indianapolis, was the sort of player who enjoyed getting sensational results even more than he enjoyed winning. For years, he tried, unsuccessfully, to score by underleading aces against suit contracts, in rubber bridge games. Just how much this cost him I do not know, but finally he struck gold. One day, he found the king in the dummy, the jack in the declarer's hand, and the queen doubleton in his partner's hand, and he was on lead against a slam contract. He underled his ace and declarer played low from the dummy, and Joe's partner actually played the queen and returned the suit to Joe's ace and trumped the third round. Joe let out a whoop like an Apache Indian and got up and danced around the room three times. Finally, all of the money he had spent and all of the time he had waited came to this supreme moment. If you, too, enjoy the thrill of a spectacular result more than you enjoy winning, I recommend you make it a habit to underlead your aces against suit contracts. It will cost you a lot of match points, or IMPs, or Victory Points, or coin of the realm, or whatever you play for, but finally it will work for you, provided only you don't lose all of your partners before that happy moment.

Emile Borel takes a look at this lead in his classic book, *The Mathematical Theory of Bridge*. He points out that the chances of success depend upon the number of cards in the suit led.

TRICKS LOST PER 100 LEADS BY UNDERLEADING AN ACE, AND BY LEADING THE ACE

Holding	Underleading the Ace	Leading the Ace
A x x	10.8	5.6
A x x x	13.3	4.6
A x x x x	17.3	4.0

If there is any lesson to be learned from Borel's table, it is that when you have a choice between underleading an ace and leading one, it is much more dangerous to underlead it than to lead it. Or you might say that it is better yet to look for another suit to lead.

EASLEY BLACKWOOD was born in Birmingham, Alabama in 1903 and learned to play bridge at the age of 11 when his parents and grandparents needed a fourth. In 1933, he created the best-known bridge convention in the world. When the ACBL was experiencing financial and administrative difficulties,

Blackwood was asked to assume the League's highest position. Within three years, he had eliminated the debt and showed a $1 million surplus. He was a very successful insurance executive, won many championships and was one of the first 500 Life Masters. His best-selling books included "Blackwood's Play of the Hand" and "Blackwood on Slams." Easley lived in Indianapolis most of his life and became one of the most respected and popular teachers in the country. He died in 1992 after a long and illustrious career.

RANDY: When I first started playing, it was always such a thrill to sit down against Mr. Blackwood. He was one of the kindest men I ever had the privilege to befriend and he always gave me wise advice in my business. I had the immense pleasure of publishing two of his books: "The Complete Book of Opening Leads," which was selected as the Book of the Year by the ABTA, and "Card Play Fundamentals" by Easley and Keith Hanson.

TWENTY-SEVEN

Do Not Underlead an Ace on Opening Lead Against a Suit Contract

"Learn the fundamentals of the game at your leisure and stick to them. Band aid remedies never last."

—Jack Nicklaus

THIS IS ONE of my favorite principles. There aren't many rules that are ironclad at bridge, rules you should follow 100% of the time. This is one of them. You have probably seen deals in a newspaper or magazine column when an expert underleads an ace on opening lead against a suit and it leads to a brilliant result. If you make this play, there are many negative possibilities. Your partner might have no idea what to play on the first trick, so the lead might not work even when a helpful card combination is present. It can destroy partnership trust and ruin the defense. A good plan: If you are defending against a suit contract with a suit headed by the ace, in most cases it makes sense to lead another suit on opening lead (Of course, there are exceptions, such as when your partner has bid the suit or you decide to make an aggressive lead such as A-x).

There is another advantage besides partnership solidarity. On hands such as the following example, you can confidently make a play at trick one so the defense is easier. By playing the jack (when you know for sure that your partner on opening lead doesn't have the ace), you can find out right away who has the queen. If declarer has it, he will win the first trick with the queen and you can look elsewhere for tricks; if declarer has to win with the ace, you will know that partner has the queen and base your defense on this fact.

The opponents have reached 4♠. Your partner (West) leads the ♥2 and you hold the K-J-6-3 as shown below. Play the ♥J to discover if declarer has the ♥Q.

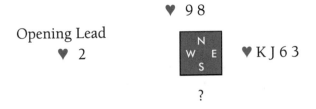

Of course, you can find examples when underleading an ace is the only winning play, but I contend that it fails more than it succeeds. Here is a hand from the March, 2018 *Bridge World* magazine. One of the world's best players had to choose a lead from:

♠ 6 2
♥ 8 4
♦ A 9 7 5 2
♣ K 8 4 3

After the auction:

Pass	1♣ Artificial and forcing
1♥ 8–10 HCP Balanced	1NT 18–19 HCP
2♣ Stayman	2♥
4♥	

It's a difficult opening lead problem and any of the four suits could be right. Thankfully for our example, he led a low diamond, underleading his Ace. Partner had a singleton diamond and the ♣A, so the ♦A or a low club would have defeated the contract. Declarer made five at this table; at the other table from the other side, the singleton diamond was led, setting the contract two tricks. The underlead of the Ace cost his team 13 IMPs.

Besides partnership confidence, here is the best reason to avoid underleading an ace against a suit contract. Let's say you underlead your ♥A against a contract of 4♠ and as you had hoped, declarer plays low from dummy:

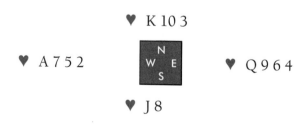

♥ K 10 3

♥ A 7 5 2   N W E S   ♥ Q 9 6 4

♥ J 8

Life would be great if partner put up his Queen, but he visualized the hand quite differently from the actual one-and played the 9. Here is what he expected the layout to be:

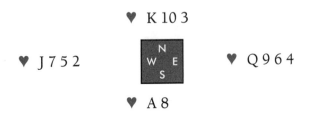

♥ K 10 3

♥ J 7 5 2

♥ Q 9 6 4

♥ A 8

It's silly for him to play his Queen on the expected hand, allowing declarer to win his ace and then finesse the 10 to take three tricks in the suit when he is entitled only to two.

By never underleading your ace, he can confidently play the 9 when it's the proper play. Simple but effective.

♠ ♡ ◇ ♣

TWENTY-EIGHT

If You Have Other Alternatives, Avoid Leading an Unsupported Ace (No King) in an Unbid Suit on Opening Lead Against a Suit Contract

"In the beginner's mind there are many possibilities; in the expert's mind there are few."

—Shunryu Suzuki

I HAVE ALREADY EXPLAINED that I never underlead an ace against a suit contract; it's one of the few rules I never violate. There's a corollary to this principle: try not to lead an ace unless you also have the king (as Easley Blackwood discussed in Principle #26). Look for a better choice among the three other suits. There's an old saying, "Aces were meant to capture kings and queens, not threes and deuces." That's why leading another suit usually makes sense.

There are few feelings more frustrating than when you lead an ace on opening lead, setting up declarer's unguarded king, allowing the opponents to make an otherwise unmakeable contract. That should be sufficient incentive to follow my rules about leading and under-leading aces against suit contracts. However, you should realize that sometimes you have clues from the bidding and the cards you hold that give you valuable evidence to the contrary. Such hints come with experience and opening leads are almost always at best an educated guess. All you can do is think about your best option instead of just throwing a card on the table. Sometimes you have two or three reasonable leads and, on a good day, all is well. On a bad day, well that's when it's good to be playing with a sympathetic partner who understands how the universe has conspired against you.

♠ ♡ ◇ ♣

TWENTY-NINE

Lead Partner's Suit

"Years ago, there were only two acceptable excuses for not leading your partner's suit: Having no cards in the suit and sudden death."

—Alfred Sheinwold

ALTHOUGH THERE ARE certainly exceptions, unless there is a great reason to break this rule, go ahead and lead your partner's suit when he has bid. Remember how important it is to have partnership cooperation, trust, and a positive relationship with the person sitting across from you. If the lead doesn't work out for the best, you can live with the result. Remember, it is possible that your result will be duplicated at other tables. Your partner might have taken a dangerous risk to enter the auction, and if so, there's nothing more frustrating than being ignored.

So I wouldn't recommend following Ron Andersen's advice in the 1979 Vanderbilt competition:

"If I told you once, I've told you three times, don't lead my suit unless I bid it three times."

Easley Blackwood asked, "When do you not lead your partner's suit?" His intelligent answer, "When you want to see what a mad partner looks like." It's true... if you lead another suit and it works, it will probably be forgotten quickly, but if leading his suit was the correct lead, he might be upset for awhile and it could affect your partnership harmony.

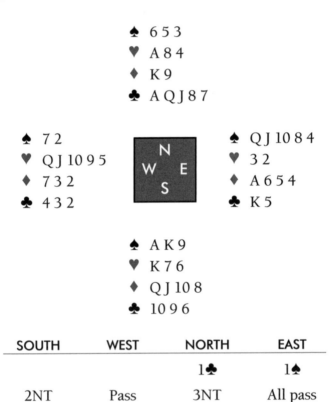

	♠ 6 5 3	
	♥ A 8 4	
	♦ K 9	
	♣ A Q J 8 7	

♠ 7 2		♠ Q J 10 8 4
♥ Q J 10 9 5	N	♥ 3 2
♦ 7 3 2	W E	♦ A 6 5 4
♣ 4 3 2	S	♣ K 5

	♠ A K 9	
	♥ K 7 6	
	♦ Q J 10 8	
	♣ 10 9 6	

SOUTH	WEST	NORTH	EAST
		1♣	1♠
2NT	Pass	3NT	All pass

This deal is a classic example of why it's almost always a good idea to lead partner's suit. When West leads the ♠7, East wins two minor suit tricks plus his three spade tricks before declarer can win nine. If the ♥Q is led, the timing shifts to declarer's advantage and he can easily win 11 tricks.

THIRTY

When the Auction Calls for It, Lead a Trump on Opening Lead

"Failure to prepare is preparing to fail."

–John Wooden

LTHOUGH VIRTUALLY every opening lead you make is at best an educated guess, it's important to take advantage of your impeccable schooling. There are many deals when a trump lead is possibly or probably the best lead; these are times when you simply should use your best judgment. However, there are three general situations that scream out for a trump lead and you should recognize them instantly on the following auctions:

1. When declarer has bid two suits and dummy takes a preference. The dummy should be short in one of the suits. This is especially true when dummy prefers the second suit.

2. When partner passes your takeout double below the three level. He should have excellent trumps and so you are hopeful of drawing as many of declarer's trumps as possible, starting with the opening lead.

3. When the opponents have sacrificed and your side possesses most of the high cards in the deck. A trump lead is usually called for to keep the declarer from ruffing some of his losers in dummy.

There are other times when a trump lead seems indicated. One case is when you want to make a passive lead so you don't help declarer.

Another occasion is when it seems declarer might want to crossruff. It is then wise to lead a trump to try to pull as many trumps as possible.

If you are aware of situations when a trump lead could be a winner, you'll definitely improve your defense and impress everyone at the table.

THIRTY-ONE

Defensive Strategy Against Notrump Contracts

"In the midst of chaos, there is also opportunity."

—Sun Tzu

MOST OF THE TIME when you are defending against a notrump contract, your primary goal is to win the race to set up a long suit (or suits) for your side and cash them before declarer can take the required number of tricks. However, there are two other strategies against notrump that can also be successful. We will discuss all three of them and look at some helpful examples and quizzes.

1. **ACTIVE.** The most common strategy is the attempt to establish *long* cards. Setting up a long suit is usually your best hope of tricks when declarer's side has most of the high cards. With the opening lead as an advantage, the defense plugs away at its longest suit at every opportunity, racing to set up long cards before declarer has the tricks he needs. Without a compelling reason to switch, the defenders will stick relentlessly to the suit they start with.

One implicit problem in this approach: Even if the defense sets up long cards, the player that has them must get the lead. Therefore, the defenders must take care to preserve an *entry* in the hand where the winners lie or will lie. This idea may affect the choice of opening leads against notrump. For example, if you hold:

♠ A 5 2
♥ 6 5 2
♦ K 10 8 5 3
♣ A 3

and you hear the opponents bid 1NT – 3NT, you routinely lead your ♦5. But with:

♠ 6 4 2
♥ J 10
♦ J 8 6 4 2
♣ 7 4 2

a diamond lead is less attractive. Even if can set up your suit, you have no way to gain the lead to cash the winners. Sometimes you should try to establish your *partner's* long suit, and the ♥J opening lead would be the choice of many players.

This deal shows how the defenders must worry about communication in notrump defense.

1.

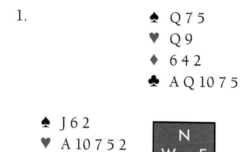

♠ Q 7 5
♥ Q 9
♦ 6 4 2
♣ A Q 10 7 5

♠ J 6 2
♥ A 10 7 5 2
♦ 10 8 5
♣ 8 3

South opened 1NT, and North raised to 3NT. West leads the ♥5. Declarer plays low from dummy, and East produces the king, winning the trick. Declarer follows low to the first heart. East returns the ♥8, and declarer plays low again. **What should West do?**

Should West win the ace and return a third heart? He can establish his suit but without an entry he can never cash the long hearts. Knowing that declarer has the ♥J and is always entitled to one heart trick, West should duck the second heart, allowing dummy's queen to win. If East wins a trick later, he can return a heart if he has one left. Then West wins and takes his long cards. To defeat the contract, West must save his entry until his suit is set up. The defenders, who have few high cards for entries, often use these ducking plays.

Suppose your partner is opening leader and has the long suit you must establish. Your objective should be to win an early trick and return your partner's lead. You must spend your entry early so you can set up his suit while he still has (you hope) an entry. Here's an illustrative deal.

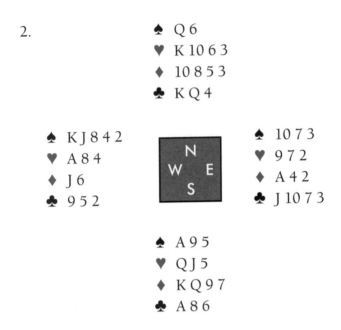

2.

♠ Q 6
♥ K 10 6 3
♦ 10 8 5 3
♣ K Q 4

♠ K J 8 4 2
♥ A 8 4
♦ J 6
♣ 9 5 2

♠ 10 7 3
♥ 9 7 2
♦ A 4 2
♣ J 10 7 3

♠ A 9 5
♥ Q J 5
♦ K Q 9 7
♣ A 8 6

You are East, defending 3NT. West leads the ♠4. Declarer puts up dummy's queen, winning, and leads a low diamond from dummy at trick two. **What must East do to beat the contract?** East must go right up with his ace. This is no time to play second hand low. East uses his entry early so he can return a spade, establishing the suit while West still has the ♥A as an entry.

What happens if East plays low and declarer scores one quick diamond trick? With one trick in the bag, declarer shifts to hearts and sets up enough tricks in that suit to make 3NT. *This type of play by East is common. It involves a basic idea in notrump defense.*

Look at this deal.

3.

     ♠ A 5
     ♥ 8 5 3
     ♦ A 8 4 2
     ♣ K 10 9 5

♠ Q J 10 7 3
♥ 9 6 2
♦ 9 6
♣ A 8 3

You are defending 3NT. South opened 1NT, and North raised. You lead your ♠Q, of course. Declarer wins the ♠A in dummy and — get ready! — leads a club to his queen. **What do you do?** If you recall the idea of clinging to your entry until your suit is set up, you will *duck* at once. Perhaps declarer's clubs are Q-x-x-(x) . Then he will probably lead a second club (you duck again) and finesse dummy's 10! Partner wins and sets up the spades while you still have the ♣A. Of course, if declarer has the ♣J, your play won't help; but if he lacks the jack, you must try to fool him.

Note that you must duck *smoothly.* If you hesitate before playing low, declarer will know what is going on. Remember, *hang on to your entry until your long suit is established.*

II. **PASSIVE.** If dummy is weak in high cards and lacks a long suit, declarer may have a hard time establishing tricks. *If the contract seems to be touch-and-go,* an active approach may lose. By leading from your honors in an attempt to set up long cards, you may give away crucial tricks. In a PASSIVE approach you try to exit *safely* whenever you must lead. Declarer may come up short of tricks, especially if you don't help him.

A passive strategy may be clear when you choose your opening lead. Look at this situation.

NORTH	SOUTH
	1♣
1♠	INT
2NT	Pass

As West, what do you lead from:

4.
♠ 8 3
♥ K 7 6 2
♦ J 9 5
♣ K 10 9 6

A case exists for a safe, passive defense. You can start by leading a spade through dummy's suit. Perhaps this is not dynamic, but it is fairly safe. Imagine how the play will go. First, the opponents *have no extra strength*, so declarer may have trouble scraping up eight tricks. He may have unpleasant guesses in choosing which suits to lead and how to attack them. Also, your black-suit holdings suggest that declarer won't take many tricks in those suits;

you have the clubs sewed up, and partner surely has at least four spades. A spade lead is unlikely to set up tricks, *but you may not need to establish long cards to prevail.* The contract may die of natural causes when declarer runs out of tricks. A heart lead may let you set up a long heart eventually, but it may give away a crucial trick in the process.

5.

    ♠ J 7 5
    ♥ A 10 2
    ♦ K 10 5
    ♣ 9 6 4 2

♠ K 8 6 4 2
♥ Q 8 5
♦ Q 6 2
♣ Q 7

You are defending 3NT. South opened 1NT, North raised to 2NT and South went on to game. Your spade lead is covered by the 5, 9 and queen. Declarer then leads a heart to the ace and a heart back to his jack. You win the queen. **What do you do?** Since dummy is weakish and lacks a long suit, go passive. Get out with your last heart and let declarer struggle with his anemic dummy. If you lead anything but a heart, you may give away a trick — possibly the ninth trick!

III. **KILLING A SUIT.** Sometimes it will he obvious that the contract will fail if the defenders prevent declarer from using his long suit. In this case, the focus shifts to an attack on declarer's *communication.* The defense must forget about setting up a suit of their own. If they can keep declarer from winning long-card tricks, he is bound to run out of high-card tricks eventually.

6.

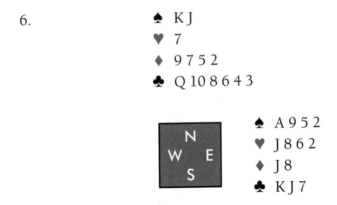

♠ K J
♥ 7
♦ 9 7 5 2
♣ Q 10 8 6 4 3

♠ A 9 5 2
♥ J 8 6 2
♦ J 8
♣ K J 7

You defend 3NT. Partner leads the ♥3 and declarer wins your jack with the queen. He cashes the ♣A, partner following low, and continues with a low club. Partner discards, and declarer plays dummy's 10, losing to your jack. **What do you lead?** Should you return your partner's lead or switch priorities? The hearts can wait, especially since partner has only four. Return a low spade, killing declarer's obvious entry to the club suit. Without club tricks, declarer will surely fail. (It's better to lead a low spade than the ace, then a low spade; save the ♠A to get in for a heart return).

The defense can also cause trouble by *holding up a winner* and ruining declarer's communication. In this deal a defender held up with *two* winners in a suit.

7.

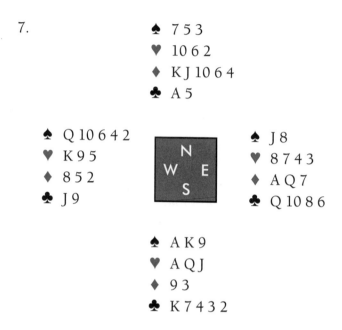

♠ 7 5 3
♥ 10 6 2
♦ K J 10 6 4
♣ A 5

♠ Q 10 6 4 2
♥ K 9 5
♦ 8 5 2
♣ J 9

♠ J 8
♥ 8 7 4 3
♦ A Q 7
♣ Q 10 8 6

♠ A K 9
♥ A Q J
♦ 9 3
♣ K 7 4 3 2

South opens 1NT, North raises to 2NT and South goes on to game. The opening lead is the ♠4. Declarer ducks East's jack, damaging the defenders' communication in *their* suit, and wins the spade return. Next, he passes the ♦9. **What should East do?**

East should *duck* the first diamond and win the second. Declarer, out of diamonds, lacks the communication to set up the diamonds and return to dummy to cash them. Note the difference if East wins the *first* diamond.

Don't forget the possibility of KILLING A SUIT in *declarer's* hand.

8.

♠ A K 4 3 2
♥ A K 6
♦ K Q 2
♣ 6 5

♠ 6 5
♥ Q J 10 7 3
♦ 7 6 5
♣ K 7 2

You are defending 3NT. North opened 1♠ and raised South's 1NT response to game. Declarer ducks your ♥Q opening and wins the continuation. He then leads a club from dummy and plays the 10 from his hand. If declarer's hand is:

♠ 7
♥ 8 5 2
♦ J 9 3
♣ A Q 10 9 4 3

or

♠ 7
♥ 8 5 2
♦ A 9 3
♣ Q J 10 9 4 3

you must refuse this trick; otherwise, declarer will bring in the clubs and make his game.

Let's review the possible strategies against notrump:

I. ACTIVE: The defenders plug away at a long suit, hoping to establish it. They must take care to *preserve an entry* to the long cards.

II. PASSIVE: The defenders try to *lead safely* and avoid giving declarer undeserved tricks. Declarer may fall short of his contract without high cards and good suits to develop. In this approach, the defenders may lead from a sequential holding, lead back a suit declarer has led first or lead a suit in which declarer clearly has strength.

III. KILLING A SUIT: The defenders try to deny declarer his best source of tricks. They attack declarer's communication by forcing out his entries prematurely and holding up their high cards.

Our last deal illustrates some of these techniques:

9.

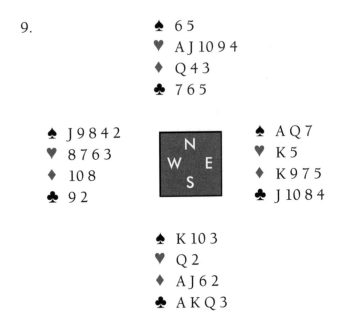

♠ 6 5
♥ A J 10 9 4
♦ Q 4 3
♣ 7 6 5

♠ J 9 8 4 2
♥ 8 7 6 3
♦ 10 8
♣ 9 2

♠ A Q 7
♥ K 5
♦ K 9 7 5
♣ J 10 8 4

♠ K 10 3
♥ Q 2
♦ A J 6 2
♣ A K Q 3

South deals and opens 1♣. North responds 1♥. South jumps to 2NT and bids 3NT over North's 3♥ rebid. West leads the ♠4. East has two winning lines of defense. The first is to play the ♠Q at trick one. This play prevents declarer from holding up his king and keeps the defenders in communication.

Even if East begins with the ♠A and ♠Q (and declarer holds off), he still has a chance. When declarer leads his ♥Q for a finesse, East must duck without batting an eyelash! Unless declarer has crystal ball, he will repeat the finesse, and now the heart suit will be lost.

QUIZ ON STRATEGY VS. NOTRUMP

1.

♠ A K 2
♥ K 10 2
♦ J 3
♣ Q J 10 8 4

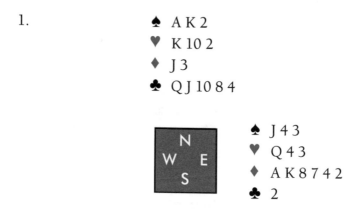

♠ J 4 3
♥ Q 4 3
♦ A K 8 7 4 2
♣ 2

You are defending 3NT. North opened 1♣, you over-called 1♦, South bid 2NT, North raised to 3NT. Partner leads the ♦9. Plan your defense.

2.

♠ 8 4
♥ 8 6 4
♦ K Q 10 5 4 3
♣ A 2

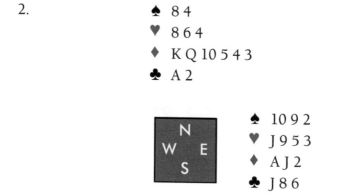

♠ 10 9 2
♥ J 9 5 3
♦ A J 2
♣ J 8 6

You defend 3NT. South opened 1NT, and North raised to game. Partner leads the ♣3, and declarer wins your 9 with the jack. Next, declarer leads a diamond to dummy's queen. How do you defend?

3.

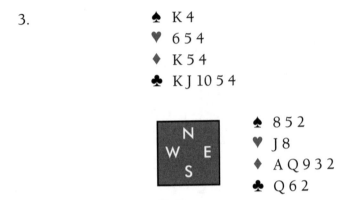

♠ K 4
♥ 6 5 4
♦ K 5 4
♣ K J 10 5 4

♠ 8 5 2
♥ J 8
♦ A Q 9 3 2
♣ Q 6 2

You defend 3NT. South opened 1NT, and North raised to game. Partner leads the ♠J. Declarer wins dummy's king, leads a heart to his ace and passes the ♣9 to your queen. Plan your defense.

4.

♠ A 4 3
♥ K J 3
♦ 7 4 3
♣ 9 6 4 2

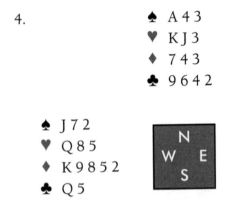

♠ J 7 2
♥ Q 8 5
♦ K 9 8 5 2
♣ Q 5

You defend 3NT. South opened 1NT, North raised to 2NT, and South went on to game. You lead the ♦5, which goes to partner's jack and declarer's queen. Declarer then leads a heart to the king and a heart back to the 10. You win the queen. How do you defend?

5.
♠ K 3
♥ Q 10 8
♦ A 4 2
♣ Q J 10 6 3

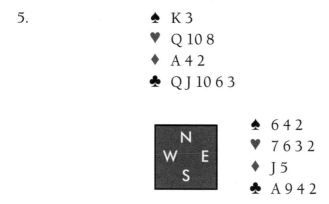

♠ 6 4 2
♥ 7 6 3 2
♦ J 5
♣ A 9 4 2

You defend 3NT. South opened 1NT, and North raised to game. Partner leads the ♣Q. Declarer wins in dummy with the king and leads a low club. How do you defend?

6.
♠ 7 5 3
♥ J 8 3
♦ K 10 9 8 5 3
♣ A

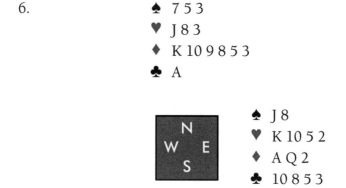

♠ J 8
♥ K 10 5 2
♦ A Q 2
♣ 10 8 5 3

You defend 3NT. South opened 1NT, and North raised to game. Partner leads the ♠2, and declarer takes your jack with the king. Declarer then leads the ♦J, playing low from dummy. You duck, and declarer continues with another diamond, partner discarding. After winning the queen on the second diamond, how do you continue?

SOLUTIONS

1. Duck the first trick. To play the ace, king and another diamond won't help because you have no entry to your long cards. You must keep the partnership communication open. Maybe partner will win a trick with the ♣A or ♣K and will have another diamond to lead. Then you can run your suit.

2. Duck the first diamond. If declarer has two diamonds, this play prevents him from setting up the suit. You retain a double stopper while declarer has only one diamond left in his hand. Killing declarer's long suit should be your goal, especially when partner is known to have only four spades.

3. Return a low diamond. Partner is marked with the ♣A, since declarer did not cash that card before finessing for the queen. In that case, partner's spades cannot be as good as A-J-10-x-x — declarer must have the ace as well as the queen. Try to beat the contract with diamond tricks instead of returning partner's lead.

4. Exit safely with a heart. With dummy so weak, and with any other return likely to cost a (perhaps crucial) trick, it's time to go passive.

5. Hop up with the ♣A to return partner's suit. You spend your entry early, trying to set up the spades while partner saves his entries .

6. Shift to a club, knocking out declarer's only entry to the diamond suit. Without diamond tricks, his chances of making the contract are slim.

♠ ♡ ◇ ♣

THIRTY-TWO

When You Are Defending, Count as Much as Possible

Counting to a bridge player is similar to an actor learning his lines...it doesn't guarantee success, but he cannot succeed without doing it.

—George S. Kaufman

COUNTING SEPARATES the average player from the good player, the good player from the very good player and the very good player from the top player. When you watch an expert who seems to know where every card is located, counting is the reason his play is so impressive. It's hard work, but a winning result isn't automatically given to you just because you sat down at the table. Counting certainly takes constant practice, but it definitely pays huge dividends in the long run. The more you do this, the better you become at it.

What should you count on every hand to have the most success possible? Start with the high-card points each player has and the number of cards he has in each suit. It's challenging because even though the bidding is over, there is more information available when each card and each

trick is played. You'll need to update the count continu-
ously. That's why most players don't form this treasured
habit: you should pay attention to everything during every
deal. It's also easy to lose concentration as the play proceeds or simply be lazy, just throw cards on the table and
take a vacation, so to speak. This can result in zero per
cent plays and embarrassing moments. We've all had those
times of being unsure which card to discard at trick 11 or
12 (which can hand declarer an impossible contract or an
undeserved overtrick).

There are two simple but crucial concepts that apply on
virtually every deal you defend:

1. YOU NEED TO COUNT YOUR TRICKS. You know
   the final contract and how many tricks you will need
   to defeat declarer. Your goal is to take enough tricks
   to make him go down. As play develops, you want to
   take as many tricks as possible.
2. To accomplish your goals, DEFEND BY ASSUMING
   YOUR PARTNER OR DECLARER HAS A SPECIFIC
   CARD OR CARDS.

It's important to realize that consistent winning defense
is impossible without counting everything throughout the
play. This includes:

a. COUNTING DECLARER'S DISTRIBUTION.
   The bidding often provides helpful clues. You'll
   learn more from partner's opening lead and count
   signals, and also when partner and declarer don't

follow suit. Before the play is finished, you may have a complete count of declarer's distribution.

b. COUNTING DECLARER'S HIGH-CARD POINTS. You'll usually have a reasonable idea of his strength from the bidding. As the play continues, you'll have more information on what cards declarer has and then you'll be able to form a picture of your partner's hand.

c. COUNTING DECLARER'S TRICKS. This will tell you whether you should adopt an active or passive approach on defense.

My goal of this principle is to help you understand that counting is the most important job you and your partner have on defense.

You not only have to count tricks, points and distribution, but while you are concentrating on that you also have to watch partner's signals, make sure you don't give declarer extra information, and play the proper card to give partner as much vital information as possible. It's easy to understand why defense is considered the most difficult part of the game to master.

QUIZ ON COUNTING ON DEFENSE

1.
    ♠ Q 6
    ♥ 10 7 4 2
    ♦ Q 10 8 4
    ♣ Q 5 2

♠ 10 8 5
♥ 8 3
♦ A K 3
♣ J 10 9 7 3

South opened 1♥ and went to 4♥ after North raised to 2♥. You lead the ♣J, which holds. Declarer ruffs the next club and draws two rounds of trumps, your partner's jack falling on the second round. Next, declarer leads the ♠Q, a spade to his king and the ♠A. He ruffs a fourth round of spades in dummy, as partner plays the jack, and ruffs a club back to his hand. Declarer then leads a low diamond toward dummy. How do you defend?

2.
    ♠ 7 6
    ♥ K 8 6 5 2
    ♦ A Q 7 6
    ♣ A 6

♠ K 9 4
♥ Q 9 3
♦ 10 4
♣ 10 8 7 4 2

South opened 1♦, North responded 1♥; South rebid 1♠, North jumped to 3♦. South bid 3NT. You lead the ♣4. Dummy plays the 6, partner wins the king and returns the ♣3, declarer following low to both tricks. At trick three declarer leads a spade to his queen, and you win the king. How do you defend?

3.

♠ K J 8 5
♥ A 10 6 5
♦ J 4
♣ A 7 5

♠ 9 2
♥ Q 7 3
♦ K Q 9 5
♣ 10 8 4 2

South opened 1♠, North raised to 3♠, South bid 6♠. You lead the ♦K. Declarer wins the ace and draws two rounds of trumps, your partner following. Next, declarer plays the ♣K and ♣A and ruffs a club in his hand. Declarer then exits with a diamond to your queen. How do you defend?

4.
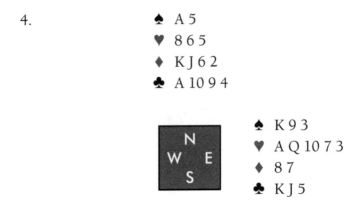

♠ A 5
♥ 8 6 5
♦ K J 6 2
♣ A 10 9 4

♠ K 9 3
♥ A Q 10 7 3
♦ 8 7
♣ K J 5

You, East, opened 1♥. South overcalled 2♦, North raised to 4♦, South went on to 5♦. Partner leads the ♥2. You win the ace, and declarer drops the king. Declarer ruffs the next heart and draws two rounds of trumps, your partner following once. South ruffs dummy's last heart and leads the ♣Q from his hand, ducking in dummy. You win the ♣K. How do you defend?

5.

♠ 10 4
♥ A J 6
♦ Q 7 5 3
♣ K J 7 5

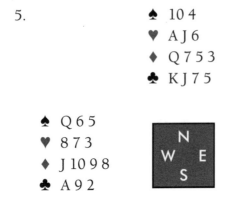

♠ Q 6 5
♥ 8 7 3
♦ J 10 9 8
♣ A 9 2

South opened 1♠, North responded 2♣; South rebid 2♥, North bid 2NT; South tried 3♠, North raised to 4♠. You lead the ♦J. Declarer wins the ace, plays off the A-K of trumps and leads another trump to your queen. Partner follows with the jack on the second trump and discards on the third. Declarer ruffs your diamond continuation and leads a club from his hand. Do you win or duck?

SOLUTIONS

1. Play a low diamond. Declarer is known to have five hearts, four spades and one club, so he has three diamonds. If he lacks the ♦J, he will probably finesse the ♦10. Note that you must do your counting in advance so you can play low without pause.

2. Declarer is marked with four clubs from partner's plays. (Partner would win the ♣Q with K-Q-3 and would return the ♣J with K-J-3). Declarer bid spades and diamonds and should have four cards in each suit; so he has at most a singleton heart. Shift to the ♥Q, in case declarer's singleton is the jack.

3. Declarer had five spades and two clubs. If he had three diamonds and three hearts, you can get out safely with a diamond. A diamond return is also safe if declarer had two diamonds and four hearts — a ruff-and-discard won't help him. A heart return runs an obvious risk, and a club return would give declarer a ruff-and-discard he could use if he had three diamonds and three hearts.

4. Count declarer's tricks. He has six diamonds and one spade. Even if you return a club and give him three club tricks, he is still a trick short and must lose a spade to you eventually. Any other return costs the contract, since declarer's hand is:

♠ Q x x x
♥ K
♦ A Q 10 x x x
♣ Q x

5. Play low, since declarer's pattern should be 6-4-1-2.

I'll close with a profound quote from Victor Mollo:

"The chances are that if you asked an average seven-year old to add five and four and one and subtract the total from 13, he would come up with the right answer. Why is it then that so many intelligent adults produce the wrong answer?"

THIRTY-THREE

After Partner Makes the Opening Lead, You Can Think About the Deal After Dummy Plays

BY VERNA GOLDBERG

"The desire to have things done quickly prevents their being done thoroughly."

—Confucius

Although it's not discussed or done often, as third hand you have the right to take some time before playing to trick one. This possibility is very seldom considered and it can make the difference between defeating the contract and allowing declarer to make it. There are a number of thoughts that can be going through your mind:

1. Reviewing the bidding
2. Analyzing the opening lead
3. Counting your possible defensive tricks
4. Your best play on this trick

5. The best overall plan to defeat the contract
6. Counting declarer's and your partner's hands
7. Thinking through all of your options together

All successful declarers stop and analyze the details before playing to the first trick and you should too, as third hand. If this process takes more time than usual, you can simply state:

"Sorry. I just need to study the dummy." Or "I have no problem; I'm thinking about the hand." Your partner will appreciate your contemplation. Both of you should make this a habit.

VERNA GOLDBERG has directed at the Louisville Bridge Center for thirty years and is the most popular teacher in Kentucky. Her priority in her classes is to impart her absolute joy of the game. She has enabled numerous students to learn "the world's greatest game" and have fun in the process.

♠ ♡ ◇ ♣

THIRTY-FOUR

Always Pay Attention to the Small Cards

IT'S ALL IN THE SMALL
BY BETTY STARZEC

"Men trip not on mountains,
they stumble on stones."

–Hindustani proverb

IN THE COURSE OF TRYING to hone my judgment skills quite a few years ago, I was fortunate to be able to partner with ACBL Hall of Fame member, Eddie Wold. While Eddie taught me many things, one of the most important he said was "It's all in the small." He had prefaced that statement with a question: "What are the most important cards in the deck?" Actually, I was astute enough to declare "The deuce!" He smiled and said "Absolutely! The most important cards are the deuces!" He referenced an out-of-print book published in 1995 by Henk Wilemsens called *It's All in the Small – How to Discover and Profit from Small Clues for Winning Bridge*.

New and advancing players may find this hard to accept with those big honor cards winning tricks. However, the key to both good defense and offense is to pay attention to the little cards; and, if you don't see those deuces ask yourself, "Why not?"

Here are a couple of examples where paying attention to the small cards gives you a winning result.

Example 1 • No one vulnerable

♠ 4
♥ A J 8 2
♦ J 8 7
♣ K 8 6 5 4

♠ 10 8 7 3 2   ♠ A 9 6
♥ 9 6 3   ♥ 10 5
♦ 5   ♦ A 9 6 4 3 2
♣ 10 7 3 2   ♣ Q 9

♠ K Q J 5
♥ K Q 7 4
♦ K Q 10
♣ A J

WEST	NORTH	EAST	SOUTH
			2NT
Pass	3♣	Pass	3♥
Pass	4♥	Pass	Pass
Pass			

West leads his singleton diamond, East wins the Ace and returns a diamond for West to ruff. This is a known singleton, because East sees all the small cards and knows West cannot be leading a doubleton or from honor third, as that would give South a singleton diamond. Not only do you know that it is a singleton, you know you can defeat the contract as long as partner returns a spade. Play the ♦9 for partner to ruff. Partner should recognize that he does NOT see any small cards, so the 9 must be suit preference for the spade suit. You defeat the contract with the ♦A, two diamond ruffs and the ♠A.

Example 2   •   N-S vulnerable

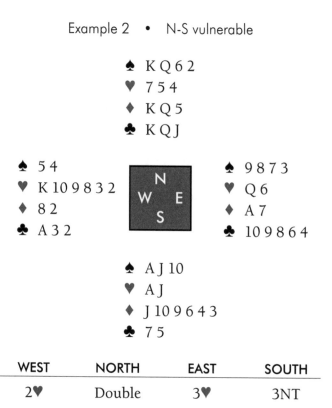

♠ K Q 6 2
♥ 7 5 4
♦ K Q 5
♣ K Q J

♠ 5 4
♥ K 10 9 8 3 2
♦ 8 2
♣ A 3 2

♠ 9 8 7 3
♥ Q 6
♦ A 7
♣ 10 9 8 6 4

♠ A J 10
♥ A J
♦ J 10 9 6 4 3
♣ 7 5

WEST	NORTH	EAST	SOUTH
2♥	Double	3♥	3NT
All pass			

193

West leads the ♥10 and East plays ♥Q. South ducks and wins the heart return. Here is where West has the chance to shine. East has an entry in diamonds, but no more hearts to lead. East needs to know where West has an entry (if any) back to the hearts. West's play to the second heart is when West can show the club entry by playing the ♥2 — the lowest spot card showing an entry in the lowest suit. You can see that without this help, East will not know whether to return a spade or a club. A spade return would allow South to make 10 tricks.

Remember it's all in the small!

BETTY STARZEC has been teaching bridge since 1985 and has taught in Indonesia, Saudi Arabia, and Japan, as well as the U.S. She is a Master Teacher with the American Bridge Teachers' Association and served as President in 2018. Betty was also the Senior Teacher Accreditation Program Trainer for the ACBL for more than 20 years. She updated the *ACBL Bridge Series* and also created the Unit Growth Seminar and other seminars for the ACBL. She is a Diamond Life Master with scores of regional and sectional wins.

THIRTY-FIVE

To Cover or Not To Cover
BY MARK LAIR

"Things take indeed a wonderous turn
When learned men do stoop to learn."

–Bertolt Brecht

WHEN TO COVER and when not to cover honors, or even 9s and 8s, in the game of bridge is a *huge* component of winning and losing. Colorful bridge expert Zia Mahmood, in very slight jest, even goes as far as saying, "when they don't cover, they don't have it!"

Here are some good examples to master, from beginner-intermediate to a more advanced level of play:

Q-J-9-x in the dummy with an unknown quantity of the suit in declarer's hand and you hold K-x-x. Do not cover. Wait for the second honor to play your king.

Declarer opens a weak-two bid and the dummy hits with Q-x-x-x. You hold the K-x over the dummy and declarer leads the queen. Absolutely do NOT cover. Give it a silky smooth duck and declarer (Zia for sure) may bounce up with the ace trying to fell the stiff king offside. They also might have J-10-9-x-x-x, lead the queen and crash your partner's stiff ace. I also recommend not covering the Q-x-x with K-x, another stiff ace possibility.

If defending against a slam, you have already cashed a sure winner and they lead the queen from Q-x-x, now you should cover from K-x. They may be trying desperately to pick up K-9-x with the stiff jack offside and your cover protects partner's J-x. A-10-8-x-x-x opposite Q-x-x would need K-9-x or K-x onside, relying on a non-cover from K-x to bring in a miracle slam!

The opponents are known to be in a 4-4 fit in their trump suit with Q-J-8-x, you hold the K-x and declarer plays the queen; smoothly duck your K-x and partner with 10-7-x must be on his toes to play the 7. With 10-9-x, partner must be even more alert and play the 9. 10-(7)-x, 10-(6)-x, and 10-(5)-x are the best examples. 10-9-x and partner could have covered to establish a sure trick. In all cases, you presume declarer (Zia for sure) will subsequently come off the dummy with the jack to pin the 10-x to his left.

A great honor-ducking situation by fourth hand (in front of the dummy): with K-10-7-x looking at the Q-J-9-x in the dummy, smoothly play the 7 on declarer's queen. After you make the smooth play, an expert such as Zia will follow up by leading his jack to pin your 107 doubleton. If you win the king on the first round, it now becomes routine for declarer to pick up the trump suit with one loser.

If the opponents have a known eight-card fit, I do not think it ever wins to cover the 9 with your K-Q-J holdings. If a six- or seven-card fit is likely, certainly you should cover the 10 or 9 from K-x, Q-x, or J-x. Covering the 10 from these holdings when your opponents are known to be in an eight-card fit is problematic. You must try to get a good feel for the given deal. Start thinking ahead at trick one and be ready for the moment!

MARK LAIR is one of the top players ever to play the game. He has won over 67,000 masterpoints, fifth all-time and was inducted into the Hall of Fame in 2009. Mark has won 22 national championships, including the Blue Ribbon Pairs with an aspiring student and another with a last-minute fill-in partner (they both played extremely well), along with a Senior Bowl World Championship.

MARK: "Including money rubber bridge and online, I tentatively claim to have played with the most partners in history. Sally, my wife of almost 50 years, has been a tower of strength in every imaginable aspect to allow me to excel in bridge."

"My son Michael gave me a special surprise two years ago at Christmas when he announced he had been studying bridge on the sly. We've been working together ever since and he has become expert-ish in the bidding. Michael, an armchair theologian with a graduate degree from Yale Divinity School, loves bridge; Sally and I hope to play with him frequently in the coming years."

THIRTY-SIX

When Declarer Leads Towards the K-Q-10-(x), Duck

"Everything you know is wrong."

–The Firesign Theater (an entertaining American comedy group that I enjoyed while in college in the early 1970s. The Library of Congress called them "The Beatles of comedy.")

THIS IS A SITUATION where many defenders err. Unless this is the setting trick, it's usually correct to play low.

There are several possible positive results when you duck:

1. Declarer might be unsure which defender has the ace and he may misplay.
2. Declarer could have entry problems and may not be able to lead a second time from his hand.
3. Even if declarer has led a singleton, this may save your side a trick. If you hold the ace in front of the K-Q-10-(X) and take the trick, declarer will have two discards on the K-Q. When you duck, the declarer wins the K or Q but then has no discards instead of two. It is important to try to have a count of the

declarer's distribution, so you will have an idea of when ducking could be the wrong play.

So when dummy appears with one of the following card combinations, your radar should tell you there is a strong possibility that you should duck when declarer leads from his hand:

K Q 10 5

K Q 6

K Q 10

K Q 5 3

This is true whether you are playing in front of or after dummy.

When you have the following situation, as West you should ready yourself to duck the second time declarer leads towards the K-Q-10-5.

K Q 10 5

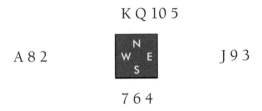

A 8 2   J 9 3

7 6 4

It's important to realize that if you are going to make this play, you should play low without hesitation. If you don't give anything away, declarer is going to guess wrong some of the time. As declarer, when you have to make this guess, the less experienced the player, the more likely he is to hop up with the ace as West.

THIRTY-SEVEN

When in Rome, Do as the Romans Do

"To the glory that was Greece and the grandeur that was Rome."

–Edgar Allan Poe

ALTHOUGH I HAVE recommended that you keep your bridge system simple, you might like to try Roman discards, also known as odd-even discards. They are helpful because you give up very little to play them as defenders. Note that odd-even signals are permitted only on the first discard.

Here is one method of how Roman discards are played:

- An ODD card encourages in the suit that is discarded. It can be a very clear signal that you like this suit. The ♥5 simply says you like hearts and would like the suit led when possible.
- An EVEN card can be used in one of two ways:

1. It is discouraging in the suit that is discarded. So the ♣2 would discourage partner from leading a club.

2. I like to play that an even card is NEUTRAL. It is
only a suit-preference discard. For example, if the
declarer is playing in spades and you discard the ♣2,
it is a preference for diamonds, the lowest-ranking
remaining suit. The ♣8, would be a preference for
hearts, the highest-ranking remaining suit.

Just as when you are playing standard signals, sometimes you aren't dealt an appropriate card. However, I have
found that there are fewer problems when I'm playing
Roman Discards because there are more options available.
After playing the system for many years, it is as comfortable as an old shoe. If you have a solid partnership, you
might want to try them.

A WORD OF CAUTION: Playing any kind of non-standard
methods (Roman discards, Upside-down count and attitude, etc.) places a burden on your partnership to try to
play in tempo as often as possible. You want to make sure
that you don't give unauthorized information to each other.

♠ ♡ ◇ ♣

THIRTY-EIGHT

Use Discretion When Signaling on Defense, Especially Against Top Players

"Discretion is the better part of valor."

—Shakespeare, Henry IV

I
T'S OBVIOUSLY IMPORTANT to cooperate on defense with partner and to give signals so you each have as much information as possible. This is true on most deals, but there are exceptions.

One situation when it is wise to keep your strategy to yourself is when it is clear that partner doesn't have any help for you. A classic example is when the opponents auction has been 1NT-3NT and you hold an opening hand or better. They have shown about 26 HCP or maybe more. Partner doesn't have many points and you are probably on your own trying to defeat this hand. You can concentrate on setting up tricks in your hand and ignore signaling. Any accurate information you give out will usually help declarer more than your side. If you are on opening lead, it's a reasonable time to consider giving a false count, such as starting with your third or fifth best card in your longest suit (if you are playing fourth-best leads).

Another situation when you should be careful not to signal is when you are playing a card that might be important later in the play of the hand. Be aware that signaling with a high card like an 8 or 9 to show partner you like a suit can sometimes cost a trick. Although they are very complicated and inexperienced players should not play them, that's one of the reasons I have recently adapted upside down signals. It's often comforting to be able to play a 2 or 3 instead of a high card to show partner you like the suit. A very large number of experts play upside down count and attitude, because there are various advantages. However, they have spent many hours perfecting their signals in these high-level partnerships. Personally, I feel comfortable playing upside down signals after experimenting with them for a few years, but I still like standard count signals.

Here's an example of a deal when signaling made life easier for declarer and enabled him to make his contract.

Both Vulnerable • Dealer South

```
            ♠ Q 7 5
            ♥ 10 8 6 3
            ♦ A Q J
            ♣ 8 7 3

♠ 10 3                      ♠ K J 9 6 4 2
♥ J 9 7 4 2       N         ♥ 5
♦ K            W     E      ♦ 10 7 6 2
♣ A J 9 5 2       S         ♣ 6 4

            ♠ A 8
            ♥ A K Q
            ♦ 9 8 5 4 3
            ♣ K Q 10
```

SOUTH	WEST	NORTH	EAST
1♦	Pass	1♥	Pass
2NT	Pass	3NT	All pass

This is from a team game and the bidding was identical at both tables. In the first match, the normal lead of the ♣5 was made. Declarer cashed ten tricks to make his contract with one spade, three hearts, four diamonds and two clubs.

At the other table, West gave the defense a chance with his ♠10 opening lead. When East signaled with the 9, he told declarer how to play the hand. South held up until the second round. He cashed three diamonds, three hearts, and put West in with the ♥10. After cashing his two hearts,

West had to give South two tricks in clubs, so the contract was successful at both tables.

At trick one, the defense would have had a better chance if East had played the J, 6 or 4. South then might have won the first trick, assuming West could have the K♠.

This hand shows how careful you should be when you signal.

One more piece of advice: When you are matched against experts, you should consider whether your signal will be more helpful to partner or to your opponent. I have regretted many times when I showed a top declarer a blueprint on how to play the deal. Like a magician, declarer conjured an extra trick or two out of nowhere, leaving me to wonder why I didn't keep the information to myself.

THIRTY-NINE

The Ideal Falsecard Can Fool Declarer Without Misleading Partner

"People are so simple and yield so easily to the desires of the moment that he who deceives will always find another who will suffer to be tricked."

—Nocclo Machiavelli

AN EXCITING and enjoyable part of defense is deception. The key to being tricky and gaining from your falsecarding is to know when use this tool. It's important to understand that there are situations when you might mislead partner and cause more harm than good. I'll discuss some situations when there is little or no chance of this, so you will know some of the best deceptive plays when you are defending.

Some players arc so eager to be tricky that they overdo it. Here is the first thing to learn about deceptive defense.

Avoid frivolous falsecards. Make deceptive plays only with a purpose.

Too often, you'll see a player indulge in something like this:

♠ 10 7 5 3

♠ Q J 4   ♠ 9

♠ A K 8 6 2

Declarer, playing 4♠ with this trump suit, cashes the A-K of trumps. West falsecards (so to speak) with the queen on the second round. This accomplishes nothing since declarer knows the situation, but East is apt to miscount declarer's distribution or the defenders' tricks.

The ideal falsecard fools declarer without fatally misleading partner.

A falsecard offers an opponent a losing option in the play or diverts him from making a winning play. One principle of falsecarding is that you can fool an opponent if you *play a card he already knows you hold (or will soon know you hold)*. Some of the following examples illustrate this principle.

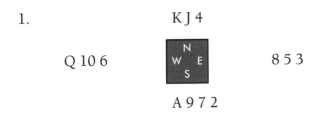

1.   K J 4

Q 10 6   8 5 3

A 9 7 2

This is a well-known falsecarding position. Needing four tricks, declarer leads low to dummy's jack, winning. When declarer cashes the king next, *West must drop his queen.*

Suppose West plays the 10 instead. Declarer now leads the 4 toward his hand and, when East follows, goes up with the ace — he knows West still has the queen. After West plays the queen, however, declarer has a losing option — he can lead low to the 9, playing West for Q-6 and East for 10-8-5-3. *Note that our falsecarding principle applies*; West can gain by playing the queen, *the card he is known to hold*, under the king.

2.

♠ J 7 4 2

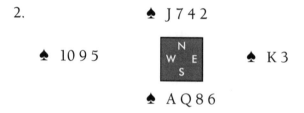

♠ 10 9 5   ♠ K 3

♠ A Q 8 6

This suit is trumps. Declarer leads low from dummy to his queen, winning. West *must* follow with the 9 or 10. Declarer now has a losing option — he can reenter dummy and lead the jack, hoping to pin West's doubleton 10-9. Note that without West's falsecard, declarer has no choice but to bang down the ace next.

3.

♠ 3

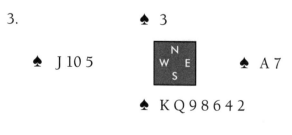

♠ J 10 5   ♠ A 7

♠ K Q 9 8 6 4 2

Declarer winds up in 4♠ after opening 3♠ with his seven-card suit. He leads dummy's 3 and wins the king when East ducks. West must follow with the jack or 10. Declarer may then continue with the queen, trying to smother the doubleton J-10 in West. Note that if West doesn't falsecard, declarer will have no options — he must lead low on the second round, hoping to bring down the doubleton ace from East.

4. A Q 7 5 2

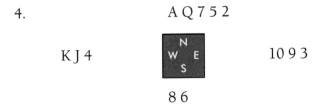

K J 4　　　　　　　　　　　　　10 9 3

8 6

Declarer needs to establish this suit at notrump. He finesses dummy's queen and cashes the ace. If West follows with the king (the card he is known to hold) on the second round, he may persuade declarer that the suit is splitting unfavorably.

These situations illustrate mandatory or *obligatory* falsecards. A defender must falsecard, else declarer is bound to make the winning play. In the next example, a defender falsecards merely to plant a seed of doubt in declarer's mind.

5. A J 7 6 4

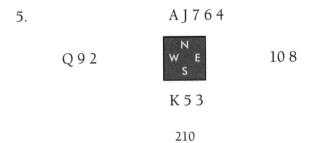

Q 9 2　　　　　　　　　　　　　10 8

K 5 3

Needing tricks from this suit, declarer cashes the king. East fears that declarer is about to finesse against West"s queen. so he drops the 10. Declarer may try to drop the doubleton queen instead or finessing.

6.   K 10 8

    A 5 4 3   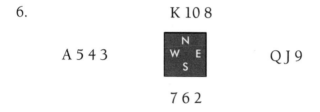   Q J 9

                      7 6 2

Declarer needs one trick from this suit. He leads low toward dummy and makes the percentage play of the 8 when West ducks. If East wins his 9, declarer has no option but to lead to dummy's king next. But East wins the jack, and declarer can then continue his plan by leading low to the 10 next.

7.   Q 9 7 6 4

    K J 10   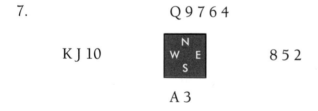   8 5 2

                      A 3

At notrump declarer considers setting up this suit. He cashes the ace, intending to lead to the queen next, hoping for a 3-3 split with the king onside. West, who sees what is coming, drops his *king* under the ace! Declarer will look elsewhere for tricks.

8.   ♥ 7 6

♥ J 9 4 2   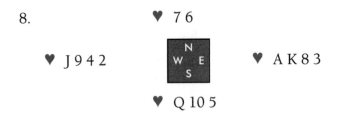   ♥ A K 8 3

♥ Q 10 5

West leads the ♥2 against notrump. East wins the *ace* and returns the 3, giving declarer a tough guess. Notice that East's play *cannot cost*. East knows that declarer has three (or more) hearts from West's lead of the 2.

9.   ♥ K Q 10

♥ J 9 4 2   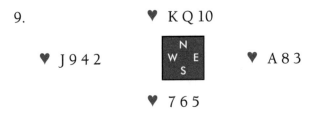   ♥ A 8 3

♥ 7 6 5

West leads the ♥2 against notrump. Declarer puts up dummy's king, and East should duck without hesitation. When West leads a heart again (or if declarer tries for a second heart trick), declarer must guess whether to play the queen or 10. Declarer can't go wrong if East takes the ace at the first trick.

Although the defenders are handicapped by not seeing each other's hands, they have a compensating advantage: they know whether declarer's finesses will work, whether his key suits will split and whether his whole plan of play will succeed.

TO REVIEW:

A falsecard offers an opponent a losing option in the play or diverts him from the winning play. Some falsecards are obligatory: unless a defender falsecards, declarer can't go wrong.

Avoid frivolous falsecards. Make deceptive plays only with a definite purpose. A good falsecard fools an opponent without fatally misleading partner. If you get too enthusiastic and falsecard aimlessly, you will have many debacles and few victories. Save your falsecards for positions you have studied.

Aside from the standard falsecarding positions, the defenders have many other chances to lead declarer astray. Some deceptive techniques are:

1. Letting declarer win the first time he tries a repeatable finesse.
2. Winning a trick with a higher card than necessary.
3. Declining to cash a winner at the first opportunity.
4. Underleading winners or intermediates to make the declarer guess.
5. Ducking deceptively.

Again, remember that a deceptive play must have a purpose. Do not play deceptive cards at random.

QUIZ ON FALSECARDS AND DECEPTION

1.

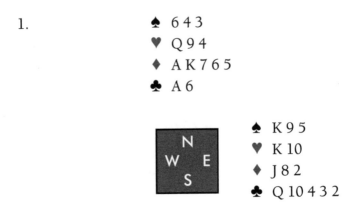

♠ 6 4 3
♥ Q 9 4
♦ A K 7 6 5
♣ A 6

♠ K 9 5
♥ K 10
♦ J 8 2
♣ Q 10 4 3 2

South opened 1♥, North responded 2♦. South rebid 2NT, North jumped to 4♥. West leads the ♠2. Declarer wins your ♠K with the ace, leads a club to dummy's ace and a heart from dummy. What do you play?

2.

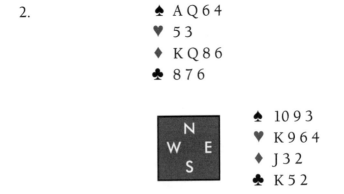

♠ A Q 6 4
♥ 5 3
♦ K Q 8 6
♣ 8 7 6

♠ 10 9 3
♥ K 9 6 4
♦ J 3 2
♣ K 5 2

South opened 1NT, North responded 2♣. South rebid 2♠, North raised to 4♠. West leads the ♣J, won by declarer's queen. At trick two declarer leads a low spade to dummy's queen. What do you play?

3.

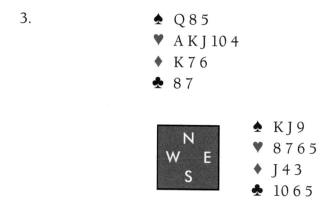

♠ Q 8 5
♥ A K J 10 4
♦ K 7 6
♣ 8 7

♠ K J 9
♥ 8 7 6 5
♦ J 4 3
♣ 10 6 5

South opened 1♠, North responded 2♥. South rebid 2NT, North jumped to 4♠. West cashes the ♣A and ♣K and shifts to the ♦10, won by dummy's king. Declarer then leads a low trump from dummy. What do you play?

4.

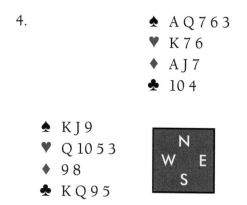

♠ A Q 7 6 3
♥ K 7 6
♦ A J 7
♣ 10 4

♠ K J 9
♥ Q 10 5 3
♦ 9 8
♣ K Q 9 5

North opened 1♠. South responded 2♣. North rebid 2♠. South tried 2NT. North raised to 3NT. You lead the ♥3. Partner plays the jack, and declarer wins the ace. Declarer then leads a spade to dummy's queen and continues with the ♠A. What do you play?

SOLUTIONS

1. Play the *king*. Declarer is likely to have A-J-x-x-x. He will win his ace and lead to dummy's 9, playing you for the singleton king and partner for 10-x-x-x. If, as expected, declarer has the missing heart honors, a falsecard is your only chance to win a trick.

2. Play the *9* (or 10). If your partner has the king of trumps, declarer will he tempted to come back to his hand and lead the jack, hoping to pin the doubleton 10-9 in your hand.

3. Play the *jack*. This will cost nothing if partner has the 10. If declarer's spades are A-10-x-x-x, he will win and lead low to dummy's 8 on the second round, playing you for the singleton jack or the doubleton K-J.

4. Drop the *king*, the card you are known to hold. You hope to persuade declarer that the spades are not splitting evenly. Perhaps he will switch to clubs.

Appendices

Dear Reader:

I've included a little bridge at the end of this volume: lists of my favorite books and a fun quiz to enjoy with your partner to see how well you really know each other. However, most of the following pages are about experiencing our magnificent globe.

It's unusual to include travel advice and stories in a bridge book, but travel and bridge have always been a wonderful combination in my life. Whenever I have attended a bridge tournament or visited a bridge club, I have always considered what journey awaited me nearby.

Because I've been passionate about travel my entire life, I have decided to share my recommendations and experiences with you at the end of this book. I hope this information will inspire you to explore our amazing planet and have your own adventures.

Here is one of my favorite passages from "The Art of Pilgrimage" by Phil Cousineau. When sculptor Henry Moore was asked if there was a secret to life, he made an astonishing reply, "The secret of life is to have a task, something you devote your entire life to. And the most important thing is—it must be something you cannot possibly do."

An impossible dream of mine is to visit every country in the world. Well, it takes three assets to travel frequently: you need enough time, enough money and good health.

Most of my life I've been fortunate to possess those three assets. My problem was (besides raising a family and running a company) that I loved going to certain areas of the world. So I got sidetracked by returning to many of my favorite places and I certainly have no regrets about those decisions. It's also exciting to have a long bucket list; I'll visit as many of those areas as possible in the coming years. May you make new friends all over the world and have safe travels,

Randy

Classic Bridge Books

I LISTED "A Few of My Favorite Bridge Books," on Page 60 in Volume 1 of "Almost the Only Bridge Book You Will Ever Need." They are repeated here for your convenience, along with my recommendations for which ones are suitable for you.

1 = Advanced Beginners
2 = Intermediate
3 = Advanced
4 = All players

1, 2	Bergen: *Points Schmoints*
1	Blackwood & Hanson: *Card Play Fundamentals*
4	Cohen: *Larry Teaches Declarer Play*
4	Cohen: *Larry Teaches 2 over 1 Game Forcing*
2, 3	Cohen: *To Bid or Not To Bid (The Law of Total Tricks)*
4	Darvas & de V. Hart: *Right Through the Pack*
4	Ewen: *Opening Leads*
1, 2	Grant: *Popular Conventions*
2, 3	Grant & Rodwell: *2 over 1 Game Force*
1, 2	Hardy & Bruno: *2 over 1, An Introduction*
2, 3	Kantar: *Advanced Bridge Defense*
1, 2	Kantar: *Modern Bridge Defense*
3	Kelsey: *Killing Defense*
2, 3	Klinger: *100 Winning Duplicate Tips*
1, 2	Lampert: *The Fun Way to Advanced Bridge*

4   Lawrence: *Dynamic Defense*

4   Lawrence: *How to Read Your Opponents' Cards*

4   Lawrence: *Judgment at Bridge*

3   Love: *Bridge Squeezes Complete*

3   Mollo: *Bridge in the Menagerie*

2, 3   Mollo & Gardener: *Card Play Technique*

3   Reese: *Master Play*

1, 2   Root: *Commonsense Bidding*

1, 2   Root: *How to Play a Bridge Hand*

4   Root & Pavlicek: *Modern Bridge Conventions*

3   Rubens: *Secrets of Winning Bridge*

4   Seagram & Smith: *25 Conventions You Should Know*

4   Seagram & Smith: *25 Ways to Compete in the Bidding*

4   Simon: *Why You Lose at Bridge*

1, 2   Stewart: *Comprehensive Guide to Defense*

4   Stewart: *Keys to Winning Bridge*

1, 2   Truscott, D.: *Bid Better, Play Better*

1, 2   Truscott, D.: *Winning Declarer Play*

2, 3   Watson: *Play of the Hand*

3   Woolsey: *Matchpoints*

3   Woolsey: *Partnership Defense*

NOTE: You cannot go wrong with any book by Larry Cohen, Audrey Grant, Eddie Kantar, Mike Lawrence, Barbara Seagram or Frank Stewart.

Below are other titles from my library that I have read and reread over the years. I consider these to be among the best bridge books ever written. Each of these either taught me much about the game or greatly entertained me. All were first published in 1990 or earlier, so many are out of print and hard to find. Some are now available in newer editions for your future enjoyment.

Blackwood, Easley. *Play of the Hand with Blackwood*. 1978
Brown, John. *Winning Defense*..................................... 1960
Coffin, George. *Bridge Play Four Classics*.................. 1975
Darvas & Lukacs. *Spotlight on Card Play* 1960
Forquet & Garozzo. *The Italian Blue Team Bridge Book* 1969
Goren, Charles. *The Sports Illustrated Book of Bridge*. 1961
Goren, Charles. *Goren on Play and Defense* 1974
Hamman, Bob. *At the Bridge Table*............................. 1994
Harrison-Gray, Maurice. *Country Life Book of Bridge*..... 1972
Hervey, George. *The Bridge Players' Bedside Book* 1964
Kantar, Eddie. *Bridge Humor* 1977
Kantar, Eddie. *Bridge Bidding Made Easy* 1978
Karpin, Fred. *The Art of Card Reading*........................ 1973
Kay, Norman, et al, *The Complete Book of
    Duplicate Bridge* 1970
Kearse, Amalya. *Bridge Conventions Complete*............ 1990
Kelsey, H.W. *Advanced Play at Bridge* 1979
Kelsey, H.W. *Improve Your Bridge* 1971
Kelsey, H.W. *Match Point Bridge* 1970
Kelsey, H.W. *More Killing Defense*.............................. 1972
Kelsey, H.W. & Glauert,M. *Bridge Odds for
    Practical Players*.. 1980
Kelsey, H.W. & Ottlik, Geza. *Adventures in Card Play* ..1979

Klinger, Ron. *Cue Bidding to Slams* 1983

Klinger, Ron. *Modern Losing Trick Count* 1987

Lawrence, Mike. *Play Bridge with Mike Lawrence* 1983

Lawrence, Mike. *How to Play Card Combinations* 1988

LeDentu, Jose. *Championship Bridge* 1974

Machlin, Jerome. *Tournament Bridge, An
    Uncensored Memoir* 1980

Mackey, Rex. *The Walk of the Oysters* 1964

Miles, Marshall. *All 52 Cards* 1983

Mollo, Victor. *Bridge Immortals* 1968

Powell, Richard. *Tickets to the Devil* 1968

Reese, Terence. *Bidding a Bridge Hand* 1972

Reese, Terence. *Play Bridge with Reese* 1969

Reese, Terence. *Play These Hands with Me* 1983

Reese, Terence. *Reese on Play* 1975

Reese, Terence & Trezel, R. *Snares and Swindles
    at Bridge* 1976

Sheinwold, Alfred. *Five Weeks to Winning Bridge* 1975

Sheinwold, Alfred. *Book of Bridge Puzzles (#1–6)* 1971

Simon, S. J. *Cut for Partners* 1950

Sontag, Alan. *The Bridge Bum* 1977

Stewart, Frank. *Better Bridge for the Advancing Player* ... 1984

Thomas, Frank. *Sherlock Holmes, Bridge Detective* 1976

Truscott, Alan. *The Great Bridge Scandal* 1969

Von Elsner, Don. *The Best of Jake Winkman* 1981

Wei, C.C. *Precision Bidding in Bridge* 1969

Do You Know Your Partner?

SO YOU THINK you know all about that person who sits across the bridge table from you? Life is too full of tests that you have to pass or suffer the consequences. However, in this test you risk nothing except your partner's wrath, and after all, you risk that every time you sit down to play. The answers aren't in this book; only your partner can tell you the correct answers. Give this short test to each other when you have a few minutes. My suggestion: the loser buys the winner a beer, a meal or pays for the next session of bridge ("Do You Know Your Partner?" was a booklet I co-authored with Andrew Bernstein 40 years ago; some of the questions are from that booklet and I added a few new ones). The scoring is simple: 1 point for each question that is answered correctly. For questions such as #2 where there are four questions, 4 points are available. HAVE FUN!!!

1. Within 3 years, how old is your partner?
2. Does your partner know the author of:
    a. Five Weeks to Winning Bridge
    b. Bridge in the Menagerie
    c. The Raven
    d. Watson's Play of the Hand
3. What kind of pizza does your partner prefer?
4. In what state or country was your partner born?
5. What kind of pet(s) does your partner have?
6. What religion is your partner?

7. What is their favorite college or professional team?
8. Has your partner been to:
   a. Europe
   b. Canada
   c. South America
   d. Antarctica
9. Has your partner ever read:
   a. Five Weeks to Winning Bridge
   b. Why You Lose at Bridge
   c. To Bid or Not To Bid: The Law of Total Tricks
10. Does your partner know who won the last NCAA basketball championship? World Series? Masters golf tournament?
11. For whom did your partner vote for in the last president election?
12. Can your partner name:
    a. The first three presidents of the United States
    b. The five Great Lakes
    c. The two most populous countries on earth
13. Does your partner favor the legalization of marijuana?
14. Is your partner in favor of the death penalty?
15. Which is the best part of your partner's game?
    a. Bidding
    b. Declarer Play
    c. Defense
    d. Turning the dummy
16. Has your partner spent more than $2500 on bridge in the last 12 months?

17. Does your partner know who the following people are:
    a. Ben Crenshaw
    b. Richard Chamberlain
    c. Leon Uris
    d. Howard Baker
    e. Ram Dass
18. Under what sign of the zodiac was your partner born?
19. Within ten pounds, how much does your partner weigh?
20. Who is the better declarer, you or your partner (no ties allowed)?
21. If your partner discovered a good friend was cheating at bridge would he:
    a. report him to the director
    b. speak to his friend
    c. ignore the situation
    d. ask him to play in the next event
22. How many years has your partner been playing bridge (within five)?
23. What is your partner's middle name?
24. Has your partner ever smoked cigarettes?
25. What are the names of your partner's children? (1 point for each one you can name)
26. What kind of car does your partner usually drive?
27. Does your partner speak a foreign language fluently?
28. Which of these three TV stations does your partner prefer to watch?   MSNBC, CNN or Fox

29. Which movie does your partner prefer? Forrest Gump or Pulp Fiction
30. Which group? The Beatles or the Rolling Stones
31. Can your partner name the capital of:
    a. California
    b. Texas
    c. Florida
    d. South Dakota
    e. Vietnam
32. How many master points does your partner have (within 20%)?

Happiness Is A Journey...

I'VE ALWAYS loved traveling. Despite the fact that half of the world is a mess with major problems of disease, poverty and selfish leaders, it's exciting to experience other cultures. They help us to appreciate our homeland and also to understand that the world's citizens are much more alike than different. It's sad that so many millions of people are intolerant and want to kill others because they use another name for God.

As St. Augustine shared, "The world is a book and those who do not travel read only a page." Mark Twain has given us many profound travel quotes and here is one of his more famous ones: "Travel is fatal to prejudice, bigotry, and narrow-mindedness, and many of our people need it sorely on these accounts. Broad, wholesome, charitable views of men and things cannot be acquired by vegetating in one little corner of the earth all one's lifetime."

I have three recommendations to help you enjoy your journeys, as well as helping you appreciate what you see (being a grateful pilgrim instead of simply a tourist):

1. As an enthusiastic bridge player, you can find welcoming bridge clubs in almost every city. Today it is easy to locate the clubs on the internet and let them know you are coming to visit and play there. I'm made many new friends and countless memories around the globe in this way.

2. There is an unmatched travel magazine that has been published for over 40 years: International Travel News. They are happy to send you a sample copy. You may call them at 916-457-3643 or go to their website: intltravelnews.com. They are a great resource if you like to venture off the beaten path and want the best information about how and where to travel outside the U.S. My other favorite travel magazine is National Geographic Traveler. For books with the best advice about Europe, find Rick Steves' guides; he is the best authority for that part of the world. The Rough Guides and Lonely Planet series of books are usually among the best available wherever you decide to go.

3. Add "The Art of Pilgrimage" by Phil Cousineau to your library. It's subtitled "The Seeker's Guide to Making Travel Sacred." After reading it, you will experience travel in an entirely new way.

I am sharing with you the following lists, as a tribute to our unique planet:

- Ten countries I have visited that are relatively easy to enjoy, whether in a group or as an individual traveler.
- Ten of my favorite destinations.
- Ten bucket list countries where I hope to travel soon.
- Very memorable travel adventures in my life.
- Some of my favorite travel quotes.

Ten Countries That Are Relatively Easy To Visit

1. **Canada**—Wherever you travel, the scenery is stunning. Whether you choose the Canadian Rockies, Lake Louise and Banff, the Maritime provinces, Quebec or Vancouver, you really cannot go wrong.

2. **Costa Rica**—It's a small country so you can visit the rainforest, go bird watching, relax on the beach or see a volcano up close. It's safe and inexpensive, although the roads are mostly terrible.

3. **Croatia**—Driving around the country felt like rural Florida to me. Split and Dubrovnik are special cities where you can enjoy the food and history. The many islands off the coast are fun destinations and Plitvice Lakes National Park is worth a stop.

4. **Iceland**—Fly into Reykjavik and after a few days there, rent a car to drive the Ring Road. There are many museums and hot springs all over the country, so you can take it easy as you admire the scenery. Some of the best waterfalls anywhere are close to the road. You can also see where Europe and North America meet at the tectonic plates that formed Iceland.

5. **Israel**—Despite the unsettling news reports and politics, it's a delight to visit and I've always felt safe there. The Old City of Jerusalem with its churches (including the Holy Sepulchre), mosques (the Dome of the Rock), the Western Wall and history is an area everyone should see. There are also the Dead Sea (with top notch hotels and an annual bridge

tournament), the Sea of Galilee, pristine beaches and Masada. You can take a lazy canoe trip down the Jordan River, visit the wineries in the Golan Heights and explore the Negev Desert in a three wheeled vehicle.

6. **Morocco**—I recommend you hire a guide or join a tour group. Highlights include the Atlas Mountains, and the entertaining cities of Marrakech and Casablanca. The culture is amazing, the food is delicious and the shopping is great fun. Staying in tents in the Sahara Desert was my highlight and camel rides are always available (make sure you hold on tight).

7. **Netherlands**—The canals, very friendly citizens, the Anne Frank house and two of the world's best art museums (Rijksmuseum and Van Gogh) are among the attractions. While staying in Amsterdam, you can take an easy day trip to see the windmills and lowlands. The tulips are a must-see in the spring.

8. **Norway**—This is arguably the most picturesque country in the world. Oslo is clean and fascinating (although expensive); don't miss the incredible Vigeland Sculpture Park there. Enjoying the fjords is sensory overload with the pristine water surrounded by forests, waterfalls and snow-capped mountains.

9. **Scotland (Great Britain)**—If you're an avid golfer, head to St. Andrews where the game started and also play the other world-class courses (Another option: you'll find hundreds of courses you haven't heard of that are inexpensive and worth a visit). There is plenty of terrific hiking and it's a pleasant country

to simply drive around to appreciate the beauty and culture. Edinburgh and its Miracle Mile are easy to navigate. You can search for Nessie at Loch Ness, Loch Lomond is a lovely area and there are castles to explore or stay in all over.

10. **Spain**—Barcelona and Madrid are among the most fascinating cities in Europe. There are many other special destinations such as Granada, Toledo and Seville. The Prado and Picasso Museums have enough masterpieces for anyone. Without a doubt, the Sagrada Familia in Barcelona is the most interesting church on earth. If time allows, the Santiago de Compostela is a hugely popular pilgrimage, ending at the cathedral.

Favorite countries I have visited:

1. **Ireland**—Every peninsula has its own personality, the Irish are a joy and it's small enough to explore easily. I love to rent a car (driving on the left isn't hard once you leave the cities) to try to find the ancient stone circles and Celtic crosses that are out in the middle of nowhere. Glendalough (founded by St. Kevin in the 6th century) is a gem with its pristine lakes and I head there whenever possible. It is my favorite site anywhere on earth. Dublin, with its pubs, historic buildings, parks and museums is one of the most popular destinations in Europe; it's a fun city to eat, drink, be merry and listen to live music.

2. **Japan**—Whatever you are searching for, the Japanese have it. The temples and forests, the food, the culture

231

and the people (who gladly solved any problem I encountered) bring me back here often. The cities are crowded but fascinating. There are several ancient pilgrimage trails such as the most popular one on Shikoku Island which I have walked three times. The baseball games are a treat, because of the enthusiasm of the fans; it reminds me of college football in the USA. Everyone should experience the Peace Park and museum in Hiroshima; despite the insanity of the war, they have rebuilt a magnificent city. There are almost 1000 sacred temples in the old capital, Kyoto; I've spent several weeks there and felt like I have barely scratched the surface. Tokyo, the current capital, mixes the ultramodern and the traditional, from the skyscrapers to its temples, palaces and gardens. In April the cherry blossoms are a real treat.

(Ireland and Japan are my two favorite countries to visit; the next eight are in no particular order).

3. **Tibet (now part of China)**—Despite the political situation in Tibet, I have visited there many times over the years. It's easy to find a company that takes groups here, especially to the capital of Lhasa. I suggest that you go there as soon as possible to experience the Tibetan culture, because more disappears every year. The rebuilt monasteries are an opportunity to see the monks debating or join them in prayer. You can still tour the Potala Museum (which used to be the Dalai Lama's winter palace), the Norbulingka (his summer palace), and the most

sacred temple in Tibet, the Jokhang in Lhasa. You can stay at Everest Base Camp on the Tibetan side or take a Landcruiser to the highest lake in the world. My favorite site (where I've trekked three times) is Mt. Kailash in the remote western wilderness. Although it's not well-known in the USA, it's considered the center of the universe for Buddhists and Hindus; it was quite a challenge for me to navigate the 19,000+ foot pass in deep snow, but these hikes have been among my most difficult and treasured accomplishments.

4. **India**—It's one of those places that is impossible to explain to someone. You simply have to go there and experience the one billion plus people and their culture. Of course, the Taj Mahal is on everyone's list. Although the Taj is incredible, I contend that the Golden Temple in Amritsar near the Pakistani border is absolutely the most beautiful building in the world when it is lit up at night. The Ganges River is crystal clear in the north where you can go white water rafting and Rishikesh is the yoga capital of the world.

5. **Mongolia**—What's not to like about a country that has almost 3 million people with only a little over 4 inhabitants per square mile? The wide-open spaces with many national parks, lakes and natural reserves make this a special area. It's not the easiest nation to travel around, but staying in comfortable yurts, meeting smiling people and praying in welcoming temples made this a memorable journey for me.

6. **New Zealand**—It doesn't get any better than this! When I returned home and was asked my

favorite area, I couldn't name one because it was all marvelous. The beaches, glaciers, wineries, hiking, penguins and outdoor sports are all world class. Our Doubtful Sound overnight cruise had countless huge waterfalls that were a highlight of our trip. There are popular bridge clubs in the cities when I wanted to take a break from the culture and beauty.

7. **Peru**—Machu Picchu is one of the most incredible sites in the world. If you are in reasonable shape and capable of a tough day hike, I highly recommend getting off the train from Cusco that takes you there. You will then be one of the few people to have the opportunity to experience the ruins from above. There is plenty more to love: the Incan capital of Cuzco, condors flying around Colca Canyon, Lake Titicaca and its floating islands, flying over the Nazca Lines and the Sacred Valley are a few of the highlights.

8. **South Africa and an African photo safari**—My wife Mary and I took this journey last year and it was awesome. We started with the country's cruel history in the apartheid museum and ended in the welcoming city of Capetown. In between, we toured three parks in Zambia, Zimbabwe, Namibia and Botswana. There were more animals and birds than I could have ever imagined: elephants, giraffes, lions, rhinos, and hippos in the wild. This was survival of the fittest at its best. I hope to see the migrations further north and the mountain gorillas in the coming years.

9. **Nepal**—This cash poor country holds a dear place in my heart; I've traveled there many times. Twice I

had the pleasure of hiking in the Annapurna region, surrounded by 20,000+ foot peaks. The trails are the same ones they have used for hundreds of years. Around the Kathmandu Valley there are countless Buddhist monasteries, Hindu temples and some of the most welcoming people anywhere. There are numerous national parks, as well as countless historical buildings. You can include Everest base camp as part of your itinerary.

10. **Georgia**—This ex-Soviet republic is very underrated as a tourist destination. They are so happy to be independent and I really enjoyed my entire time there a few years ago. Tbilisi, the capital, is a lovely combination of the ancient and the modern world. Highlights of the country include the cave churches, the monasteries, the wineries and the beauty of the mountain villages.

Ten Bucket List Countries Where I Hope To Travel Soon

1. Bhutan
2. Iran
3. Sri Lanka
4. North Korea
5. Madagascar
6. Kenya
7. Vietnam
8. Ethiopia
9. Papua New Guinea
10. Antarctica

Ten Very Memorable Travel Adventures

1. **Summer, 1967**—Because my parents trusted me (what horrible judgment!), they allowed me to take a road trip with a childhood friend from Louisville to the West Coast. At the time I was a pretty normal, straight-laced, upper middle class, Jewish 18-year-old. We had quite an experience in the six weeks we were on the road. We got very drunk on Bourbon Street in New Orleans, had our room searched by the police in Oklahoma (they were looking for drugs and all we had were switchblades we had bought), hung around the bars in the border towns of Mexico, and at the end of the trip we lost all of our money in the Nevada casinos. In between, we had quite an eye-opening time in California, listening to music and partying on Laguna Beach with the hippies and Hell's Angels, and then getting ripped off in Haight Ashbury several times by the drug dealers. To summarize how naïve we were, in Southern California they asked us: "Well, do you want to smoke some grass or drop some acid?" and we really didn't know the difference. We were fortunate to avoid falling over the cliffs near the ocean and killing ourselves, as we hallucinated and came down from our experience. Fifty years later, I have gone back several times to read my journal and laugh out loud at that crazy journey and how insane it was. I'm glad I was a perfect role model for my children ("Do as I say and not as I did" was my mantra to them).

2. **Israel, 1993**—The Maccabiah Games held in Israel every four years are the Jewish Olympics. There were competitions in a wide range of sports and games which included bridge. Over 5000 participants came from 48 countries. I was named the non-playing captain of the bridge team; my role was to go to meetings, raise money and choose a team. I was fortunate to have five world class players: Mark Cohen, Ralph Katz, Brad and Mike Moss and Howard Weinstein. We won a bronze medal after losing to the host team and outscoring a world class Canadian team. Besides enjoying much of the country, the highlights were the opening and closing ceremonies. This is one of the few places in the world where an American team could receive a standing ovation from thousands of spectators as we marched into the stadium behind our flag. These were moments I'll never forget! We had the added fun of trading pins and uniforms with many other nations, concluding a totally positive trip. Little did we know that four years later at the next Maccabiah Games, a bridge would collapse and several people would die.

3. **Miracle In Vrindavan, India, October 6, 2000**—I survived the local monkey temple in the morning when one of the resident monkeys jumped on my back, trying to steal my glasses or my camera. Luck was with me, because he just left dirt marks on my shirt; he didn't scratch or bite me. Another lady in our group wasn't so fortunate. A monkey grabbed her glasses and ran away with them. A local man was able to throw sticks at the animal and retrieve the

glasses. The most difficult part of the temple visit was not stepping in the monkey urine since you are required to take your shoes off to enter.

After buying a few statues on the street and taking our lunch break, the next stop was the fascinating Hare Krishna Temple in Vrindavan. I was barefoot again here. They were washing the marble steps and it was like skating on ice. My feet flew out from under me and I fell, hitting the back of my head on the top one. My wife Mary and two other people saw me fall down the stairs; they swore they saw blood all over me. When I stood up, I felt my head and it was fine. Somehow there was no damage to my body; the only casualty was my broken video camera. I was laughing with gratitude as we entered our bus to leave, thanking my overworked angels who had protected me from a terrible injury.

4. Mr. Goodwrench In Latvia, September 27, 2001

Panevezys, Lithuania—Today I suggested to my wife Mary that we take a day trip into Latvia from Lithuania; with misgivings, she agreed and she lived to regret this decision (although I enjoy telling this story).

The day started normally enough. On the way out of town towards Riga, the capital, we stopped again at the Hill of Crosses. It's one of my favorite sites with thousands of crosses of every size and kind; the Soviet Union bulldozed the crosses time after time when Lithuania was a Soviet republic. Eventually, Mikhail Gorbachov stopped this practice. After strolling around a Latvian palace, my plan was for us to drive through the countryside, eventually seeing the Baltic Sea and several other sites of interest.

Our problems started with a supposedly routine stop to refuel. After we filled up, a few miles down the road, Mary noticed the engine was acting strangely and the car stopped dead. When the attendant had pumped our gas, he had used diesel instead of regular gas, a prescription for disaster. We were out in the boondocks where they were plowing the fields, far away from civilization. We decided to push the car to the highway a few miles down the road. Somehow, I survived without having a heart attack and the guy who put gas in acted like he didn't understand English; he certainly didn't want to take any responsibility. A kind man in a truck roped our car to his vehicle and he drove us to a service center out in the middle of nowhere. Incredibly, it was a sophisticated garage, just like an American Mr. Goodwrench in the middle of Latvia.

At the garage, they spoke no English and as they took out the back seat and worked on the car for hours, I wondered if I'd have to buy the rental company a new car. There were other grim possibilities: they couldn't fix it and we were stuck here...they would charge us a fortune for their work...they made the problem worse since they might not understand what had happened. In the end, all was OK; they charged me $21 and I gave him $60 gratefully. The truck driver received a $20 thank you and they were all happy with the final outcome.

Then we filled the tank ourselves, having learned our lesson.

Our difficulties weren't over yet. The check engine light kept coming on (it turned out this was a false alarm). Not paying attention, I drove well past the speed limit in Lithuania, going 70 MPH in a 40 MPH zone; the police stopped me and wanted $100 in Lithuanian money. I had none and offered them dollars which they declined. I imagined spending a few days in the nearby jail or worse. But they were reasonable and allowed the ignorant Americans to go on their way. Then I offered them a bunch of basketball cards, because I knew Lithuanians were huge fans of the game. They took most of the cards I had, thanking me, but disappointed I didn't have any Michael Jordan cards to offer them. We stayed in a comfortable hotel and not behind bars that night.

5. **Annapurna Insanity, October 8, 2002 Kaski, Nepal**—I awoke at 6:00 A.M. for a crazy day that my travel company had planned. I had requested a "not-too-difficult" trek in the Annapurna area, arguably the best trails in the world.

The shepherds, goat herders and virtually all the people who bring animals through the mountains use the same routes as they walked hundreds of years ago. The paths consist of thousands of steps; eventually, the trail went almost completely uphill and it took a huge toll on me, but I continued slowly, along with my guide. After stopping for lunch, we were making our way up the mountain when a group of about six donkeys started towards us. Several passed by when suddenly one came right at me. I was near a ravine and had absolutely nowhere to go. He ran over me; he knocked me over with such force that I went completely backwards and I knew I was in major trouble. We were over a day from the nearest road, so it's not the place to have a major injury. The crown of my head hit the stones hard. My left arm and shoulder also crashed into the stones (At this time, I had a really bad shoulder that almost caused me to cancel the journey). My bag and valuables went flying over the ledge (it could have landed hundreds of feet down, but happily it was lying nearby).

I thought my arm and shoulder were broken, because of the sudden, intense pain and my prior issues on my left side. I also thought I had busted my head open on the rocks. To my absolute amazement, I was actually OK! My knee bothered me later in the day, but it proved to be nothing terrible. Somehow angels, spirit guides, God or some benevolent force gave me a reprieve from an impossible situation. In many ways, this was similar to my accident in India in 2000.

October 9, 2002: Granruk, Nepal—I was still too stubborn to turn around. The next day my guide and I decided that I should rent a horse. We thought that would be easier than walking. However, there were a few problems: it had rained heavily during the night, the horse was really a pony (used to Nepali riders half my size) and I am a hopeless horse person. The horse, Setti, was reluctant to go forward because the trail was steep and wet. He slipped and fell, luckily not on top of me. It took over an hour to free his legs. During his ordeal, I sat there praying he was all right and wondering what they would do if he wasn't (they shoot horses, don't they?). After this incident we turned around; I had finally learned my lesson.

Several years later when I was in better shape and returned to the region with my son Dustin, I was ready for a less stressful trek in the Annapurna area. We survived the ten days without any catastrophes. As we reached the place where I had rented my horse on my previous trek, Setti was grazing peacefully in the pasture. I was able to take a memorable photo with him for posterity, happy that he was healthy and ready for other riders.

6. **Mad Dogs And Tibetans, October 17, 2002**
Darchen, Tibet—Along with my guide and driver, after five days our Landcruiser arrived in Western Tibet. My plan was to trek around Mount Kailash after spending a few days relaxing and readying myself mentally and physically for the journey. This pilgrimage is called the Kora by the Tibetans. It's 32 miles around the mountain and because of the unpredictable (sometimes extreme) weather and 19,000+ foot pass, most people take three or four days to complete the trail. Despite being a very sacred area, the town of Darchen is rundown with trash everywhere. It exists because of the cheap guesthouses and restaurants for visitors who aren't camping out. As I looked around, it reminded me of an old Western town in the U.S. that was on its way to becoming a ghost town. However, there is an

incredible view of the holy mountain from the town and if you look in the other direction you see another sacred mountain 80 miles away, Gurla Mandhata. It's over 7700 meters high (over 25,000 feet) and appears that it's just next door.

I had a free afternoon, so with the weather cooperating (sun and cloudless blue skies welcoming me), it seemed like a perfect few hours to sit around and write in my journal. So I paid for some bread and along with the peanut butter I had brought as my staple, it was time for a picnic. I walked a few hundred yards outside the entrance to Darchen and I was in the middle of nowhere, completely by myself.

It was so peaceful and I couldn't keep a smile off my face, as I realized how lucky I was. This was an experience that very few people ever have; what a special time for me! I was content, alone with a magnificent view of the mountains without a care in the world.

My only problem was that a pack of 75 to 100 dogs walked into the area where I was sitting. I realized that if they wanted to come over and attack me, I had absolutely no defense. My angels were working overtime, because even though I had food, they continued on their way, not bothering me at all. Later, I had the thought that if they had decided they were hungry and wanted me for a meal, it is possible no one would have ever figured out what had happened to me. The best chance would have been if someone found my journal and clothes, but who knows how it would have played out. Being bitten by a rabid wild dog was another possibility. I'm just very thankful that the pack of dogs wasn't hungry, they had learned to ignore people or they didn't think I'd make a satisfying meal. I had survived to continue my adventure.

7. **Thank God For Sports Cards, St. Petersburg, Russia August 19, 2007**—Although this country has many of the most incredible museums, churches and palaces (The Hermitage, Peterhof, the Kremlin Armory, etc.), we couldn't wait to leave. If you are going to Russia, I suggest you join a group tour; being on our own (we might have been unlucky, but I don't think so), we met unfriendly, rude and unhelpful people everywhere we went.

Even though we are experienced travelers, it's easy to let down your guard for a few seconds. As we were attempting to return to our hotel, Mary and I entered the metro (subway) as we had done many times before. A gang of three guys and a woman trapped me and started a commotion. Before we realized what had happened, they had me cornered, acting like they were having a huge fight among themselves. How many times had we been warned about scams and problems in Russia (it really is like the Wild West with virtually no police to help)?

This could have been a complete financial disaster, because I didn't trust leaving money and credit cards in the safety deposit box in our Russian hotel. We were headed for Tibet in a few days to take a group through the country and our travel agent insisted that we deal only in American dollars. I had about $15,000 in my shoulder bag, along with credit cards and passports. These thugs could have done anything: they could have injured us severely and taken everything we had on us, including our jewelry.

The happy ending to the story is that they thought they had picked my pocket and taken my credit cards. Luckily, I always take sports cards to give to the children (and sometimes adults) when I travel. Instead of my credit cards, they managed to steal about ten basketball and soccer cards. My angels were again working overtime on my behalf.

8. **Smuggling Cheese and Walnuts, September 8, 2011 Sofia, Bulgaria**—My wife Mary and I bought train tickets in our reserved compartment (six seats), traveling from Sofia to Belgrade, Serbia. The day was like a Grade B movie unfolding in front of us. As we arrived a man was unscrewing the light on the ceiling; we naively assumed that he was a maintenance man from the railroad. There were about a dozen Serbs who routinely smuggled high-quality Bulgarian cheese and walnuts into their country; they brought screwdrivers that fit perfectly into the fixtures on the ceiling and garbage bags full of product. They had about 40 containers of cheese, hidden in luggage, under the seats and in the light fixtures. The walnuts were everywhere and some of the bags broke so the nuts were spilled onto the floor. They had worked in Bulgaria for a month and bought the contraband that they could sell for a large profit.

There were various problems with their plan. The most important was the massive number of customs agents who knew all the tricks of trade and inspected the train throughout the day.

The atmosphere wouldn't have bothered us too much (it was quite an interesting situation) except our traveling companions were among the nastiest people I have ever met. The couple started to beat up on each other (he started choking her) and even though there were "No Smoking" signs posted, when we pointed that out they ignored us and blew as much smoke as possible in our direction. When we complained to the conductor, he shrugged his shoulders and greeted us with, "Welcome to Serbia." Mary and I spent most of the trip in the hall outside our compartment; we decided we didn't want to make these people too upset at us (no telling what they might have done). I am happy to report that when we stopped at the next town, the customs people took most of their goods along with the smugglers in our compartment. We were able to relax and enjoy the rest of the ride in blessed peace and no smoke.

Wise Travel Quotes

"Whoever created the world went to a lot of trouble. It would be downright rude not to go out and see as much of it as possible." —Edward Readicker-Henderson

"A good traveler has no fixed plans and is not intent on arriving." —Lao Tzu

"An inch of surprise leads to a mile of gratefulness." —Brother David Steindl-Rast

"As you grow older, you'll find the only things you regret are the things you didn't do." —Zachery Scott

"At the end of all our exploring will be to arrive where we started and know the place for the first time." —T.S.Eliot

"Cover the earth before it covers you." —Dagobert D. Runes

"Do not seek to follow in the footsteps of the men of old, seek what they sought." —Basho

"Everything sacred moves in a circle." —Black Elk

"He who returns from a journey is not the same as he who left." —Chinese proverb

"I am astonished by people who want to 'know' the universe when it's hard enough to find your way around Chinatown." —Woody Allen

"I have found out that there ain't no surer way to find out whether you like people or hate them than to travel with them." —Mark Twain

"If traveling was free, you'd never see me again." —Anonymous

"If you reject the food, ignore the customs, fear the religion and avoid the people, you might better stay home." —James Michener

"It is good to collect things, but it is better to go on walks." —Anatole France

"It's not the road ahead of you that wears you out; it's the grain of sand in your shoe." —Arabian proverb

"Life is not a journey to the grave with the intention of arriving safely in a pretty and well-preserved body, but rather to skid in broadside, totally worn out and proclaiming: Wow, what a ride." —Anonymous

"Not all who wander are lost." —J.R.R. Tolkein

"One's destination is never a place, but a new way of seeing things." —Henry Miller

"So shut up, live, travel, adventure, bless and don't be sorry." —Jack Kerouac

"Stranger pass by that which you do not love."
—Phil Cousineau

"Stuff your eyes with wonder. Live as if you'd drop dead in ten seconds. See the world. It's more fantastic than any dream made or paid for in factories." —Ray Bradbury

"Take only memories. Leave nothing but footprints."
—Chief Seattle

"The pleasure we derive from journeys is perhaps more dependent on our mindset than the destination we travel to." —Alain de Botton

"The real voyage of discovery consists not in seeking new landscapes, but in having new eyes." —Marcel Proust

"The traveler used to go about the world to encounter the natives. A function of travel agencies now is to prevent this encounter." —Daniel J. Boorstin

"There is only one journey. Going inside yourself."
—Rainer Maria Rilke

"To wander is to be alive." —Roman Payne

"Travel far enough, you meet yourself." —David Mitchell

"Travel has a way of making the world a much smaller place."
—Janna Graber

"Travel makes a wise man better but a fool worse."
—Thomas Fuller

"Travel makes one modest. You see what a tiny place you occupy in the world." —Scott Cameron

"Wherever your journey takes you, there are new gods waiting there with divine patience—and laughter."
—Susan M. Watkins

"With age, comes wisdom. With travel, comes understanding." —Sandra Lake

"You must go to adventures to find out where you belong."
—Sue Fitzmaurice